Roberta's

CARLO MIRARCHI, BRANDON HOY, CHRIS PARACHINI & KATHERINE WHEELOCK
ART DIRECTION BY RYAN RICE

CLARKSON POTTER/PUBLISHERS
NEW YORK

Published in the United States by Clarkson Potter/
Publishers, an imprint of the Crown Publishing Group,
a division of Random House, Inc., New York.
www.crownpublishing.com
www.clarksonpotter.com

CLARKSON POTTER is a trademark and POTTER with
colophon is a registered trademark of Random House, Inc.

Library of Congress Cataloging-in-Publication Data
Mirarchi, Carlo.
   Roberta's / Carlo Mirarchi, Brandon Hoy, Chris
Parachini and Katherine Wheelock.
      pages   cm
   Includes index.
   1. Pizza.   2. Roberta's (Restaurant)   I. Hoy, Brandon.
II. Parachini, Chris.   III. Wheelock, Katherine.   IV. Title.
   TX770.P58M57   2013
   641.82'48—dc23   2013004300

ISBN 978-0-7704-3371-0
eISBN 978-0-7704-3372-7

Printed in China

Book design by Jennifer K. Beal Davis for Ballast Design
Cover design by Ryan Rice

10 9 8 7 6 5 4 3 2 1

First Edition

All photographs are copyright by the following contributors : **Neanna Bodycomb**: 288; **Anthony Falco**: 11 (right), 14–15, 19 (top right), 20–21, 22 (top left), 101, 110, 192–193 (middle), 223, 259 (bottom right), 285; **Flora Hanitijo**: 68–69; **Brandon Hoy**: 10 (left), 19 (middle left), 22 (bottom right), 23 (top right, middle center, middle right, bottom right), 50–51, 76 (top right, middle left), 98 (right), 157, 225 (bottom), 260 (middle right), 275 (middle left), 279 (top left, bottom), 280, 287; **Greg Minig**: 43; **Carlo Mirarchi**: 210, 279 (middle right); **Damian Neufeld**: 232–233; **Steve Perriloux**: 234–235; **Dave Potez**: 2–3 (bottom), 6–7, 10 (right), 13, 19 (bottom right), 46, 47, 52, 54–55, 58–59, 70–71, 76–77 (top right,

middle three right, bottom three right), 81, 86, 89, 90, 104, 107, 108–109, 113, 114, 119, 120, 123, 128, 133, 136, 138–139, 141, 143, 145, 146, 150, 154–155, 158, 162, 164–165, 168, 171, 172, 175, 180, 185, 186, 189, 191, 192 (left), 193 (right), 195, 196, 200, 202, 205, 206, 209, 214, 217, 218, 219, 225 (top), 227, 228, 230–231, 237, 238, 241, 247, 248–249, 251, 255, 259 (bottom left), 260 (top right, bottom right), 267, 268, 271, 272, 275 (top right), 277, 278; **Austin Rhodes**: 1, 4–5, 60–61, 84–85; **Ryan Rice**: 8, 16, 19 (top left, bottom left), 30–31, 44–45, 63, 76–77 (top left, top third in from left, bottom right), 82, 124, 127, 149, 242; **Roberta's**: 252, 259 (top right); **Eric Safyan**: 24–25, 29, 36–37,

259 (top left, middle right), 260 (top left, bottom left); **Ryan Slack**: 98 (left); **Hannah Spinelli**: 22 (middle right); **Nathanael Staneck**: 275 (top left); **Kenji Takigami**: 93, 94, 102, 131, 135, 167, 177, 179, 263; **Joe Talman**: 2–3 (top), 19 (middle right), 22 (top right, middle left, middle right), 34, 39, 40, 78, 212, 259 (middle left), 275 (middle right, bottom), 279 (middle left); and **Michael Harlan Turkell**: 260 (middle left). The following illustrations are copyright Roberta's: **Anthony Falco**: 279; **Benjamin Haft**: 22; **Roberta's**: 64; and **Andrew Steiner**: 26, 161. The remaining illustrations are copyright by the individual contributors: **Anthony Falco**: 42, 57, 286; **Marilee Grashin**: 48; and **Zachary Kinsella**: 117.

To the staff at Roberta's, past and present

CONTENTS

INTRODUCTION

In the summer of 2007, we put a seed in the ground. We had a simple and not at all original idea: to open a pizza place. What maybe distinguished the idea at the time was where and how we wanted to open that pizza place—in a cinderblock warehouse in a neighborhood that was wild western enough that we could afford it and, more important, that we could do almost whatever we wanted.

How we wanted to open our pizza place was on our own, with almost no money except what little we had saved and some donations from friends and family who had even less experience opening restaurants than we did. We weren't chefs. We weren't front-of-house managers. We weren't in any kind of restaurant scene. We didn't even like going out to eat—we didn't think of it as something fun to do. We were musicians and bartenders with at best a year or two of line-cook work between us. There were no investors or backers to answer to—which on the occasions when we didn't have any money at all, and they were many and strung together, seemed like something worth regretting—but it was the best thing for us. It was the only thing. We wouldn't have worked with anyone who had enough money to make opening a pizza place in Bushwick anything but hard, and they wouldn't have worked with us.

The summer before it had a name, Roberta's was a really fun place to hang out. And a comforting place to hang out if you didn't have a job or anywhere else to be or any idea what you wanted to do with your life. So a lot of people came to help us with our demolition derby. Strip the walls and fix holes. Salvage building materials. Move piles of rubble around until we could figure out how to get rid of them. Build a pizza counter. Build a bar. When there are a lot of people around, there are a lot of ideas. Which is probably how there came to be a kiddie pool in the backyard and a chicken

called Chicken and an injured dove that went by Motherfucker. When there are a lot of people around there is a lot of creative energy and a lot of exuberance. There is also a lot of noise and mess and conflict. Bones were broken and faces got swollen and people threw up. We can't think of a good thing that's happened that didn't involve some of that.

By the time the restaurant opened, in the cold, dark heart of January, what we had was a family. And a drafty, ramshackle house for that family to live in. Maybe we should have realized that all the bullshitting around it felt like we'd been doing—during and in between the genuinely hard work of building the restaurant—had been laying the groundwork for the kind of place we wanted to be. Roberta's was a place people wanted to hang out.

The rest isn't history. The rest is still happening. The seed sprouted and began to grow. And as anyone with a houseplant or a pet or a kid knows, living things are really needy. We had a family to feed. And a house to maintain. We had amazed ourselves with what we could do and we wanted to do more and we wanted to do it better.

If you've been to the restaurant more than once, you probably saw physical evidence of all that growth and change with your own eyes. Roberta's has always been pretty transparent. We like to think that is part of its charm but we know it could just as easily be called a flaw. Has been, actually. It doesn't really matter because we couldn't have done it any other way. It is less that way now. We have an infrastructure that we didn't have in the beginning. That infrastructure is supposed to save us from ourselves. But the truth is that if we'd had an agenda or anything resembling an infrastructure when we started out, we never could have created the place that we did or achieved the things we achieved. Had we any self-consciousness or any sense of limits or any inhibitions, we would have failed.

None of this is to say that we got where we are now by accident. We worked hard to get our food and the experience of eating it to a place where we feel like we can compete with anybody. Where we feel like we can legitimately compel someone to travel a good distance to see us, possibly wait an hour or more to sit, and it will be worth it. We worked incredibly hard, and we still work hard, to balance what's expected of us with what we actually want to do, to appreciate what we created and the people who help keep us in existence, without sacrificing too much of the spirit in which the place was built.

To experience Roberta's, you have to visit it. That's the truth. We realize that truth isn't unique to us, but we thought about it a lot during the making of this book. We wanted to convey the experience of being at Roberta's to those who haven't been, and capture it for those who have been too many times to count. In the end we decided that eating the food and drinking the drinks and having a good time is a much better way to get a sense of what it's like at Roberta's than reading too much about it. So there are a good number of photographs in this book. A lot happened and still happens at Roberta's that's best told visually. And of course there are some stories. Enough to give you a sense of the place and to give you context for the food and drink but not so many that you begin to wonder why we thought you'd be interested. And there is a lot of food. So cook the food, drink some cocktails or whatever you like drinking, hang out with some friends, and have a really good time. That's all we're ever trying to do.

THE FOOD

It's impossible to overestimate what the best version of a vegetable, fish, or meat can mean in cooking. We are talking about a really good variety or breed that's in peak season and absolutely perfect condition. We know how that might sound—either obvious or obnoxious. But we'll say it again: Ingredients are beyond important. So this is not a cookbook full of substitutes. We would rather frustrate you with a few ingredients that are difficult to find than frustrate you by supplying substitutions for half of the ingredients in a recipe, making you feel like what you're about to make is probably half as good as it should be, which would probably be true.

Roberta's started out with a beautiful pizza oven. So we had good pizza early on—after an amount of tinkering with the starter and the dough and the cheese and the sauce that would be boring to read about if we recounted it in detail. The pizza we serve now traveled some distance to get where it is. The food we serve that isn't pizza has traveled a long, long road. In the beginning, before we had gas and water, a lot of that food was made in Carlo's apartment, somewhere in Manhattan, and brought back to life under the buzzing glow of a toaster oven.

The way that we make our food changed over the course of five years as though decades had elapsed. But the philosophy behind the food didn't change at all. Whether you call it Italian or American or seasonal, or point out Japanese or Spanish influences, the food at Roberta's is simple. Not simple in an apple-pie kind of way, but simple in this kind of way: Here is an incredible ingredient that's been cooked and accompanied in such a way that you can taste exactly what it is. In fact, what it is has been chiseled around, concentrated, and enhanced so that it's the best version of itself.

So we won't ask you to make a lot of sauces or garnishes or side dishes meant to go with something in this book. We will ask you to seek out the best possible ingredients you can find. We will encourage you to be the asshole who gives the guy at the farmers' market 50 cents to bite into a couple of his apples before you buy them. And to peel back the husk of the corn and sink a tooth into a kernel to make sure it's juicy and sweet, not starchy, before you take it home. We will suggest that you get your hands on some specific heritage breeds of animals that have been raised on small farms, and fish that's going to be difficult to find at a suburban fish market. (We've looked.) But we will give you all of our sources (see page 282). And we will suggest the best substitutions possible where it makes sense.

We want you to have a good time cooking from this book. We want to get you excited about some really good ingredients and help you find them. We want to teach you a couple of techniques—how to make pizza dough that's the platonic ideal of chewy and flavorful, how to apply a frightening amount of heat to a tender young vegetable and not destroy it—that you'll make your own. If you're going to cook extensively from this book, there are a couple of things you might want to have on hand first: Diamond Crystal kosher salt (the kosher salt measurements in this book are specific to Diamond Crystal). Good white balsamic vinegar. Tipo 00 flour. Nice aged Parmigiano-Reggiano. Beyond that, it would be helpful to have access to a good farmers' market. And an Asian market. A supplier, nearby or online, of sea urchin roe and American caviar. The end of that list starts to sound like a letter to Santa, but you get the idea. Put the effort into getting the best stuff you can get to cook with, and put less effort into cooking. If you do that, the side effect will be that you have fun, which hopefully won't require any effort at all.

It felt like the real Thanksgiving. It was the day after the actual holiday and we were in New Haven, Connecticut, having spent the day before with family and adoptive family. We were sitting at a table at Frank Pepe, a nearly hundred-year-old pizzeria where people line up outside waiting for a table and for good Neapolitan pizza baked in a coal-fired oven. You can't manufacture the vibe going on at Pepe's. It's just a pizza place. But the energy level in that pizza place is incredible. People are eating. People are drinking. People are talking. People are happy. Guys who know what they're doing are sliding peels in and out of a massive oven at an almost metronomic pace. The pizza arrives. The pizza is good. No one wants to leave. We didn't want to leave. Sitting there that day, we decided that that was the kind of place we wanted to build. And there was no way to build it but around pizza.

In early 2007, when we started building the restaurant there, Bushwick still felt relatively lawless. There was no foot traffic on the streets. There was wind and chain-link fence and graffiti. There was exhaust from Mack trucks and wafts of corn from a tortilla factory and the constant roar of planes lifting off from LaGuardia. At night there were slow-moving garbage trucks and that's about it. But as desolate as the place looked from the outside, it turned out things were happening inside. Deep in some of the huge vacant spaces, art kids were living and working. The people we met didn't give a shit about being cool or going out to cool places. They were busy actually creating things. Coming from Williamsburg, which was way past blown up at that point, Bushwick felt real and fresh and full of possibility.

PIZZA

It wasn't random that we decided to open a pizza place. We wanted our place to be fun. We think eating pizza with your hands is a lot of fun. The plan was never to bill ourselves as artisanal or to talk on the menu or out loud about our method and the ingredients we used. We couldn't think of anything less fun than that. We were just going to put some time and sweat into making our pizza really good. That was the plan. Once we got to a good place—a pliable, flavorful crust, a sauce that did its job exactly right, and mozzarella that was the perfect balance of creamy and salty—we started messing around.

We're not the first people to have messed around with pizza. There are more bastardizations of traditional pizza in the world than there are actual bastards. But we had some rules. We used seasonal ingredients because when you're looking around for good ingredients, they're usually the ones that are in season. We didn't put barbecued chicken on our pizzas and we never let anyone sprinkle brown sugar on one (every now and then someone in the pizza kitchen really wants to do that).

We like to think we never did anything just for the sake of novelty, and that the only pizzas that went on the menu were the ones that actually tasted good. That's probably debatable. But for the most part, as in so many other parts of the restaurant, giving experimentation in the pizza kitchen a wide berth paid off. The pizzas in this chapter are here because they are some of our best, and also because they're different enough from one another that each is an opportunity to learn something. But beyond these, we encourage you—it's mandatory, actually—to mess around.

THE OVEN

There is way more fear and loathing around making good pizza at home than there needs to be. It is not that hard to make good pizza at home. It is admittedly hard, if not impossible, to make pizza at home that's exactly like it is at Roberta's. That's because the fall before we opened, after waiting months and months for some Italians in some shipping port somewhere to get their shit together, a big, beautiful pizza oven arrived in a shipping crate on our doorstep. Or, to be precise, near our doorstep.

The reason you can't make pizza at home exactly like it is at Roberta's is because we have that oven. That oven gives our pizza its wood-fired char and wood-fired flavor. That oven cooks our pizzas so fast that the crust doesn't have time to lose moisture—it stays tender and chewy. You can't make wood-fired pizza at home (unless you have a wood-fired oven). But you can make really good pizza. Setting aside the degree of heat and how you apply it, good pizza is about good ingredients. You can make quality, flavorful dough at home. You can top it with sauce and cheese you made yourself and whatever other ingredients you like, hand-selected by you. If you do all of that, your pizza is going to be good.

The only other thing you have to do is not to listen to anyone who tells you what a fool's errand it is to try to make really good pizza at home. Don't invite those people to dinner.

PIZZA DOUGH

It took a very long time to get the pizza dough at Roberta's right. And we still tinker with it. Our pizza crust reaches back to some Italian traditions but it's not classic Neapolitan by anyone's definition. A true Neapolitan pie is so waifish that you have to eat it with a fork and knife. We think eating with your hands beats eating with a fork. So while our pizza is relatively thin, the crust is sturdy and chewy. You have to work with dough a few times to get a feel for how the way you handle it affects the texture. By combining yeast with flour and water, you create a living thing. Being a living thing, your dough is going to react to actions. Beat it up and it's going to make your life really difficult. Stretch it against its will and it's going to toughen up. But handle it like a newborn baby and it's going to go pliable in your hands.

As for the flavor of the dough, that will depend on whether you make it using a natural starter—a culture of wild yeast kept alive with regular feedings of water and flour—or commercial yeast. Any starter will make your dough more flavorful than commercial yeast. That's because in a starter, yeast is reproducing, eating and digesting the sugars in the flour and producing carbon dioxide, which is the leavening agent in dough. Coexisting with the yeast is bacteria, which eats the sugar that the yeast can't digest and produces acids that give the dough flavor. We use a starter culture from Ischia, a volcanic island off the coast of Naples famous for its wild yeast starter cultures. You can buy a dried starter culture like that (and activate it with water and flour), or you can use any sourdough starter. You can borrow some from a generous baker or a friend. Two pizza dough recipes follow: one that uses a sourdough starter and one that uses commercial yeast. Your options for commercial yeast are fresh or active dry. Fresh yeast, also called cake yeast, makes for dough that's arguably a little more flavorful, with a better, springier texture than active dry yeast. We like it. Note: If you can't find fresh yeast at the supermarket, you can buy it online. It must be kept refrigerated and should be used within a week or two of purchasing. If all you can find is active dry yeast, that's fine. It's an acceptable alternative and even a good idea if you're brand new to making pizza dough.

PIZZA DOUGH WITH SOURDOUGH STARTER

MAKES 2 (240-GRAM/
8½-OUNCE) ROUNDS OF
DOUGH, ENOUGH FOR
2 (12-INCH) PIZZAS

250 grams (1¾ cups)
fifty-fifty blend of 00
flour and King Arthur
all-purpose flour

8 grams (scant
2 teaspoons) fine
sea salt

8 grams (1½ teaspoons)
good olive oil

150 grams (⅔ cup)
lukewarm water

95 grams (3½ ounces)
sourdough starter
(recipe follows)

In a bowl, thoroughly combine the flour and salt and make a well in the center. In a separate bowl, thoroughly combine the olive oil and lukewarm water and mix in the starter. Pour the wet mixture into the well in the dry mixture and begin mixing the two together with your hands, gradually incorporating the dry into the wet. This process will be more like mixing than kneading. After about 3 minutes, when the wet and dry are well combined, set the mixture aside and let it rest, uncovered, for 15 minutes. This allows time for the flour to absorb the moisture.

Flour your hands and a work surface. Gently but firmly knead the mixture on the work surface for about 3 minutes. Reflour your hands and the surface as needed. The dough will be moist and sticky, but after a few minutes of kneading it should come together into a smooth mass. Divide the dough into 2 pieces, shape them gently into balls, and wrap them tightly in plastic wrap. Refrigerate the dough for at least 24 and up to 48 hours before using. This process, called proofing, allows for the fermentation that gives the dough structure—which means a chewy, pliable crust—and flavor.

starter

To get dough to rise and form a crust, you need some sort of leavening agent. Until sometime in the mid-1800s, when commercial yeast became prevalent, leavening was done using natural starter. Commercial yeast ruled thereafter because it produces very consistent results—invaluable if you're producing a large volume of bread. At the restaurant, we use both. This recipe is for natural starter, which is all you need if you're cooking at home, where consistency isn't so crucial. Like anything alive, starter asks for some caretaking. But once you get it going, you can refrigerate it and start feeding it again only when you need to use it.

1 (6.8-gram/¼-ounce) package dried sourdough starter culture

170 grams (scant 1¼ cups) all-purpose flour, plus more as needed

170 grams (¾ cup) lukewarm water, plus more as needed

In a 1-liter (or 1-quart) glass jar, combine the starter with the flour and water and mix with a fork to combine. Cover the jar by laying a towel over the top of it or by setting a lid on top without screwing it tight. Put the jar in as warm a place as possible—ideally 75°F to 100°F. You can do this in a water bath brought to that temperature or in an oven set to the lowest possible temperature, ideally 100°F. Let it stand for 12 hours, and then feed the starter with 115 grams (¾ cup plus 1 heaping tablespoon) flour and 115 grams (½ cup) lukewarm water and cover it loosely. Now that you've started it, you can stop using a water bath or the oven and keep it in a room-temperature environment, provided it's not inordinately cold.

Continue to feed the starter as described above every 12 hours until it's airy and bubbly throughout, which shouldn't take more than a couple of days. When it becomes bubbly within just a few hours of a feeding, discard 1 cup of the starter and feed it once more. Cover it with a towel or lid as previously, and let it rest on the counter for a few hours before refrigerating.

Starter kept in the refrigerator should ideally be fed once a week (as in the last step, above, discard 1 cup and add a mixture of about 1 part water to 1½ parts flour), but it can survive for up to a month without feedings. Just know that it will take at least two cycles of feeding to reactivate it before you use it.

PIZZA DOUGH WITH STORE-BOUGHT YEAST

MAKES 2 (240-GRAM/
8½-OUNCE) ROUNDS OF
DOUGH, ENOUGH FOR
2 (12-INCH) PIZZAS

306 grams (2½ cups)
      fifty-fifty blend of 00
      flour and King Arthur
      all-purpose flour

8 grams (scant
      2 teaspoons) fine
      sea salt

4 grams (scant
      1 teaspoon) fresh yeast,
      or 2 grams (scant
      ½ teaspoon) active
      dry yeast

4 grams (scant
      1 teaspoon) good
      olive oil

202 grams (1 cup minus
      1 tablespoon)
      lukewarm water

In a bowl, thoroughly combine the flour and salt and make a well in the center. In a separate bowl, thoroughly combine the yeast, olive oil, and lukewarm water. Pour the wet mixture into the well in the dry mixture and begin mixing the two together with your hands, gradually incorporating the dry into the wet. This process will be more like mixing than kneading. After about 3 minutes, when the wet and dry are well combined, set the mixture aside and let it rest, uncovered, for 15 minutes. This allows time for the flour to absorb the moisture.

Flour your hands and a work surface. Gently but firmly knead the mixture on the work surface for about 3 minutes. Reflour your hands and the surface as needed. The dough will be moist and sticky, but after a few minutes of kneading it should come together into a smooth mass. Divide the dough into 2 pieces, shape them gently into balls, and wrap them tightly in plastic wrap. Refrigerate the dough for at least 24 and up to 48 hours before using. This process, called proofing, allows for the fermentation that gives the dough structure—which means a chewy, pliable crust—and flavor.

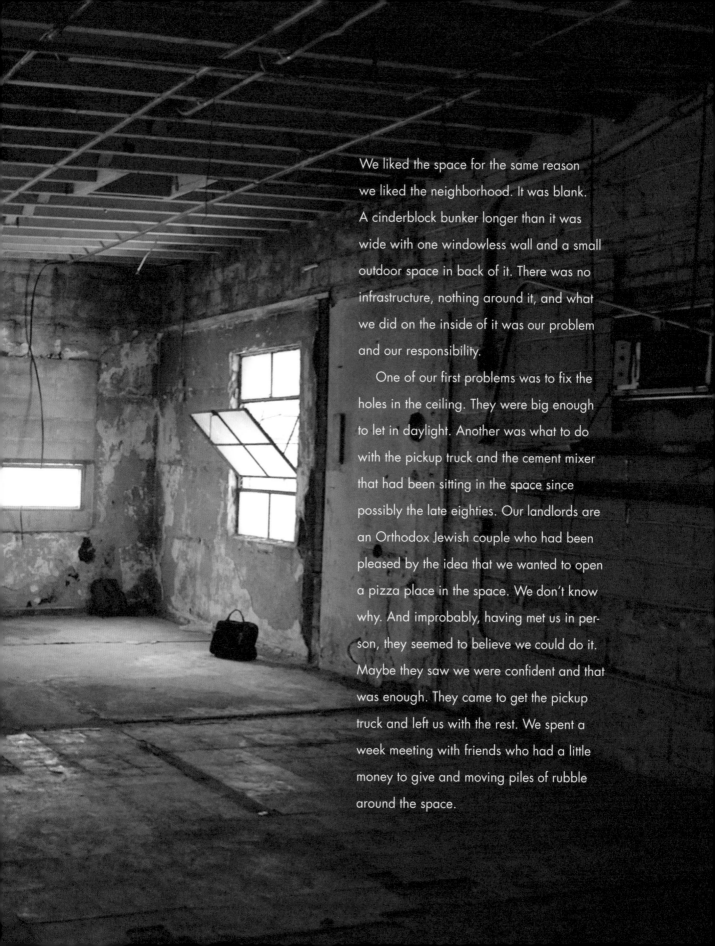

We liked the space for the same reason
we liked the neighborhood. It was blank.
A cinderblock bunker longer than it was
wide with one windowless wall and a small
outdoor space in back of it. There was no
infrastructure, nothing around it, and what
we did on the inside of it was our problem
and our responsibility.

One of our first problems was to fix the
holes in the ceiling. They were big enough
to let in daylight. Another was what to do
with the pickup truck and the cement mixer
that had been sitting in the space since
possibly the late eighties. Our landlords are
an Orthodox Jewish couple who had been
pleased by the idea that we wanted to open
a pizza place in the space. We don't know
why. And improbably, having met us in person, they seemed to believe we could do it.
Maybe they saw we were confident and that
was enough. They came to get the pickup
truck and left us with the rest. We spent a
week meeting with friends who had a little
money to give and moving piles of rubble
around the space.

HOW TO MAKE A PIZZA*

* This method is the one you should use for all of the following pizza recipes. The specific instructions for shaping and baking aren't repeated within each recipe for topped pizza.

Preheat the oven to the highest temperature, ideally at least 500°F. Place a pizza stone or, even better, four 6 × 6-inch unglazed quarry tiles, on the middle rack of the oven. The advantage of the tiles is that they're much cheaper than a stone and if they break, they're easily replaced. You can get them at places like Home Depot or, near us, from our friends at the Brooklyn Kitchen, an excellent kitchen store and cooking school in Williamsburg. Let the oven heat up for 1 hour.

Remove the dough from the refrigerator and let it come to room temperature. Lightly flour your hands and a work surface. Using your fingertips, push down any bubbles in the dough. Then use your fingertips to push down on the round of dough, from the center out to the perimeter, to encourage it to spread out. Don't *push* the dough out—any pushing or pulling you do to it will cause it to toughen, which is something to keep in mind throughout this process: Be gentle with the dough. If you push it too hard or overstretch it, you can't just re-form it into a ball and reshape it. It will become stiff and hard to work with and you'll have to toss it out and use a new ball of dough. So take your time. Spend a minute or two gently flattening the dough ball into a disc shape before you move on to the next step.

Before we explain "slapping out," which is the final step in shaping the dough (and that's really what the process is called, even by Neapolitans), a note: We spread our dough out pretty thin. We can do that because we're cooking pizza at a very high heat—800°F to 900°F. The result is thin but chewy. At home, if you spread your dough extremely thin, you'd end up with a cracker-crisp crust. That's because you'll be baking it at a lower temperature for longer, which gives it time to dry out. At home, too-thin crust is also prone to holes and to getting soggy from toppings. Aim for a round that's no bigger than 12 inches across and no less than ⅛ inch thick in the center; it should be a little thicker than that at the edges.

"Slapping out" the dough is what you could also call letting the crust form itself. It lets gravity do the stretching and shaping of the dough. There are lots of different ways to do this, and you should experiment to find the way you're comfortable with. This is the way we do it: Pick up your disc of dough and hold your hands parallel to the floor. Then squeeze your fingers together and curve them so that your hands are like paddles. Drape the dough over one hand and flip it over to the other hand in a smooth motion. Continue moving the dough slowly back and forth, rotating it 90 degrees every few seconds so that you end up with a circle. It will start to stretch. After 1 to 2 minutes, you should have a round of dough that's about 12 inches in diameter. Transfer it to a floured pizza peel—preferably a metal one—and gently push out any edges that need pushing to make a better-looking circle.

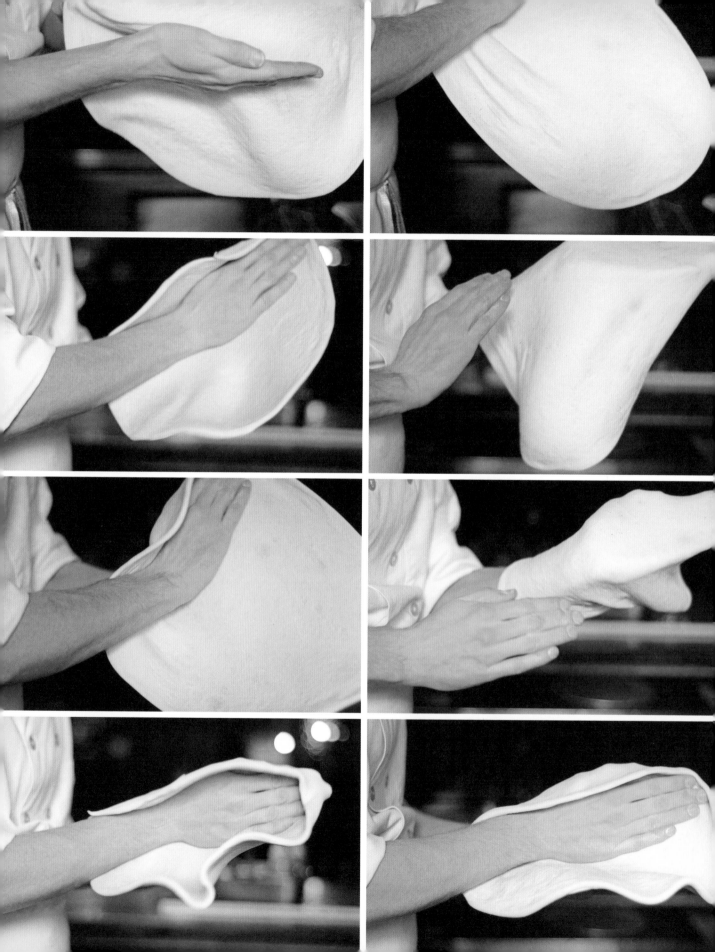

We don't ever oil the dough before adding toppings—it prevents the sauce from melding with the crust, which is what you want. Top the dough immediately after transferring it to the peel so that it doesn't start to stick, and pop it in the oven the moment it's topped; it will get soggy otherwise.

Carefully slide the topped pizza onto the stone and bake it for 5 to 7 minutes, until the crust is bubbling up and beginning to turn golden. The cooking time will vary depending on your oven and other factors (how much you've been opening the oven, for instance). Keep an eye on it. Then turn on the broiler and broil the pizza for 1 to 2 minutes, checking it to make sure the cheese doesn't brown, until the crust is golden and just starting to char in a few places. If your oven doesn't have a broiler, just cook the pizza a minute or two longer, until the crust is nice and golden. Serve it hot.

A last note on toppings: Balance in pizza topping is all about moisture. If you have a sauceless pie, you have to think about where the moisture on your pizza's going to come from—an extra drizzle of olive oil, a little more cheese. If you have a pie with sausage and cheese on it, you don't need that finishing drizzle of olive oil—you've got enough fat to add moisture. If you make pizza often enough, you'll start to get a feel for balance. The proportions for cheese and sauce in the recipes here are what we consider ideal for a 12-inch pizza. If your preference is different, or if your pizza is smaller than that, if your cheese is wetter, if you have a heavier hand with olive oil—all of that will affect the balance of the toppings. Use the proportions we call for as a guideline but be prepared to adjust and experiment as you go.

When you talk numbers in terms of building a restaurant, you're talking about so much more than money. You're talking numbers of hours, days, missing pieces, men down, permits to get, trips to Oriental Lumber for screws. At the risk of sounding like a grandfather recounting the 2,360 shoeless steps it took him to get to school every day, we went to Oriental Lumber 96 times the summer of 2007 because we never had enough cash to buy more than 200 screws at once. Running out of money happened a lot. Scavenging and stealing happened a little. We went out looking, not knowing what we were looking for, and brought back stuff that spoke to us. The light fixtures that we made by Frankenstein-ing working parts onto busted ones still light the restaurant. A pile of shitty bricks we stole from a dumpster eventually became the pizza counter. A lot looks useful to you when you don't have much.

MARGHERITA

tomato, mozzarella, basil

This is a classic margherita. As much as we've tinkered with the pizza dough over the years, we haven't messed with this formula.

Preheat the oven to the highest temperature possible. Place a pizza stone or tiles on the middle rack of the oven and let it heat up for 1 hour.

Put the sauce in the center of the dough round and use the back of a spoon to spread it evenly over the pizza, stopping about half an inch from the edge. Drizzle a little olive oil over the sauce and scatter the basil on top. (We put the basil under the cheese so that the heat from the wood-fired oven doesn't incinerate it. If you prefer, you can scatter it over the cheese, but we've grown to like it this way.)

Break the mozzarella into several large chunks and distribute it over the pizza. Bake the pizza until the crust is golden brown and bubbly.

MAKES 1 (12-INCH) PIZZA

1 (12-inch) round of pizza dough (pages 32–35)

43 grams (3 tablespoons) sauce (recipe follows)

Some good olive oil

4 or 5 basil leaves, torn into pieces

80 grams (2¾ ounces) fresh mozzarella (recipe follows)

sauce

**MAKES ABOUT 350 GRAMS
(1½ CUPS)**

1 (794-gram/28-ounce)
can San Marzano
whole peeled tomatoes

Some good olive oil

Fine sea salt

The recipe for this sauce is simple. All that matters is that you use the best-quality canned tomatoes you can find. Depending on where you are, that might mean San Marzanos or it might mean tomatoes from California or Mexico. Try a few different labels before you decide on your go-to. Some are sweeter, some are more acidic. And often the flavor of one kind varies from year to year. We like a subtle sweetness, good acidity, and strong tomato flavor.

Drain the tomatoes and discard the juice (or use it for Bloody Marys). Use an immersion blender or a regular blender to puree the tomatoes until almost smooth.

Add a splash of olive oil and a pinch of salt, blend until smooth, and taste. Add more olive oil and salt to taste, if needed, but keep in mind that the sauce will reduce a little bit when it's baked on a pizza, so it will only get saltier. The sauce will keep in the refrigerator for up to a week, and up to 6 months in the freezer.

fresh mozzarella

Nothing's as fresh as when you make it yourself from scratch. But we realized early on that the process of making mozzarella from milk—first making curd and then making cheese from that curd—wasn't going to fly with the volume of pizza we were doing. But making mozzarella straight from curd still lets you get your hands dirty and control things like salinity and texture, and it's much faster.

Break up the curd into small pieces and spread them out on a sheet pan. Let the curd come to room temperature. It's crucial that the curd be truly room temperature when you combine it with the hot water in the next step; otherwise it will lower the temperature of the water and the curd won't melt quickly enough to form the mozzarella.

Put 360 grams (1½ cups plus 1 tablespoon) water in a small saucepan and set it over high heat. When the water is just boiling, add 14 grams (1 tablespoon plus 2 teaspoons) salt. Turn off the heat and use a thermometer to check the water temperature. It should be 190°F when you combine it with the curd. Water that hot is actually painful to hold your hands in. Rubber gloves will help a little. But the water has to be as hot as possible for the curd to melt quickly. If the curd doesn't melt quickly, the mozzarella will be tough, or won't come together at all.

In a large bowl, combine the 190°F salted water with the curd and start mixing the curd and water together with your fingers. As the curd becomes more elastic, you'll be able to gently fold the pieces of it into one another. Gradually work the pieces of curd, stretching and folding and incorporating the pieces into one another, until the curd comes together in a smooth mass. (If you work the curd too much, the cheese will toughen up, so work quickly. The whole process should take about 3 minutes.)

When you have a ball formed, fill a container that's just large enough to hold it with cold salted water (5 grams/1 teaspoon of salt to 225 grams/1 cup of cold water). Transfer the mozzarella to the water to let it cool. If you're using the cheese that day, leave it out, sitting in the water, until ready to use. If you're using it later, cover the container and refrigerate it until you're ready to use it. It will keep in the refrigerator for a week.

**MAKES 454 GRAMS
(1 POUND)**

454 grams (1 pound)
      mozzarella curd*

Water

Kosher salt

* It will take a little looking, but you can buy mozzarella curd at specialty cheesemongers and online. If the smallest quantity of curd you can find is 5 pounds instead of 1, you can freeze the curd you don't use and use it later.

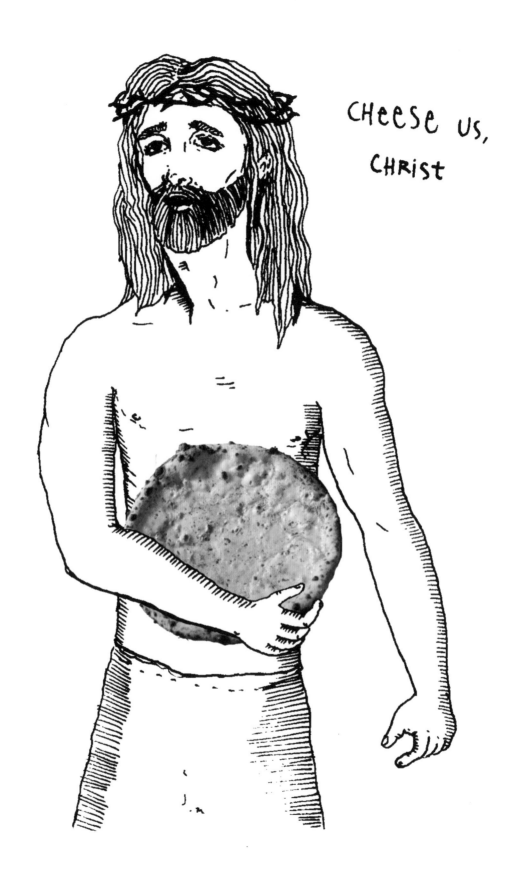

CHEESE US,
CHRIST

CHEESUS CHRIST
mozzarella, taleggio, parmigiano, black pepper

This pizza pays homage to *cacio e pepe*, the classic Roman dish of spaghetti with a lot of parmigiano, a little butter, and an insane amount of freshly ground black pepper. To turn it into a Cheesus H. Christ, which might actually edge out the original in a popularity contest, finish it with a drizzle of honey.

Preheat the oven to the highest temperature possible. Place a pizza stone or tiles on the middle rack of the oven and let it heat up for 1 hour.

Drizzle the heavy cream over the dough. Break the mozzarella into several large chunks and distribute it over the pizza. Break the Taleggio into pieces and do the same. Give the pizza 8 to 10 grinds of black pepper. Bake the pizza until the crust is golden brown and bubbly, and finish it immediately with the parmigiano.

* Taleggio, which is from the Lombardy region of Italy, is a really pungent but actually mild and buttery-tasting soft cheese. It's harder to find than it should be (see sources, page 282). If you can't find it, go to a nice cheese shop and ask for an approximation of it.

MAKES 1 (12-INCH) PIZZA

1 (12-inch) round of pizza dough (pages 32–35)

20 grams (4 teaspoons) heavy cream

60 grams (2 ounces) fresh mozzarella (page 47)

40 grams (1½ ounces) Taleggio*

Freshly ground black pepper

30 grams (1 ounce) parmigiano, finely grated

The fall before we opened, the venue for a Todd P show fell through. Through a friend of a friend, we got a call about renting our space. Within a few hours, porta potties were rolling in and kids were lining up outside. Literally a thousand people showed up for that show. They filed through the front door of the cinderblock bunker, picked their way around that pile of bricks, and climbed through a gaping hole in the wall into the empty space next door. There were slabs of plywood covering holes in the floor, pieces of ceiling hanging down, and construction debris in the middle of the dance floor. It was our first party and it went off.

GUANCIALE & EGG
tomato, mozzarella

MAKES 1 (12-INCH) PIZZA

---

1 (12-inch) round of pizza dough (pages 32–35)

43 grams (3 tablespoons) sauce (page 46)

80 grams (2¾ ounces) fresh mozzarella (page 47)

20 grams (¾ ounce) guanciale, very thinly sliced

Some good olive oil

1 large egg

This is a really good pizza but it isn't an off-the-wall original. Eggs have been put on pizzas before. The main reason it's included here is so we can explain the best way to put an egg on a pizza. Which is something you should try if you haven't.

Preheat the oven to the highest temperature possible. Place a pizza stone or tiles on the middle rack of the oven and let it heat up for 1 hour.

Put the sauce in the center of the dough round and use the back of a spoon to spread it evenly over the pizza, stopping about half an inch from the edge. Break the mozzarella into pieces and distribute them over the pizza, leaving a space in the middle where the egg will go. Distribute the guanciale over the pizza in the same way. Give the pizza a small drizzle of olive oil and bake it until the crust is golden brown and bubbly.

While the pizza is cooking, coat a sauté pan lightly with olive oil and set it over medium heat. Crack the egg into the pan and cook it without moving it until the white just barely sets. The white should be set, but the yolk should still be runny. When the pizza is done, slide it out of the oven and put the egg on top.

BABY SINCLAIR
cheddar, parmigiano, kale, maitake, garlic, calabrian chili

It's not every day that a new addition to the pizza menu becomes a fixture on the roster. The appeal of this one depends on what you like—sharp, tangy cheddar, the kick of southern Italian chilies, or maitake mushrooms, which, browned in a hot pan (or a wood-fired oven) taste unbelievably meaty. We like it all.

Preheat the oven to the highest temperature possible. Place a pizza stone or tiles on the middle rack of the oven and let it heat up for 1 hour.

Tear the kale into pieces a little bigger than bite-size, put them in a bowl, and dress with a splash of olive oil and a pinch of salt. Set aside.

In a large sauté pan coated with olive oil and set over almost high heat, sauté the maitake pieces until they begin to brown at the edges. Don't move them around too much or they won't get a chance to brown. Add a splash of vinegar and let it cook off for 30 seconds. Remove from the heat and set aside.

Pull the stems off the chilies and roughly chop them. Break or cut the cheddar into small chunks, about ¼ inch.

Scatter the garlic over the dough. Follow it with the kale, which should cover the round in a thick layer (don't worry if it looks like too much—it will shrink down in the heat of the oven). Distribute the maitake over the kale and follow it with the cheddar. Scatter the parmigiano on top and, lastly, the chilies. Bake the pizza until it's golden brown and bubbly.

MAKES 1 (12-INCH) PIZZA

1 (12-inch) round of pizza dough (pages 32–35)

A big handful of lacinato kale,* ends trimmed, ribs removed

Some good olive oil

Kosher salt

62 grams (2 ounces) maitake (hen of the woods) mushroom, trimmed, cleaned, broken into pieces a little bigger than bite-size

A splash of Banyuls red wine vinegar or sherry vinegar

5 grams (⅛ ounce) jarred Calabrian chilies**

31 grams (1 ounce) Prairie Breeze cheddar***

Half a garlic clove, peeled and very thinly sliced

18 grams (½ ounce) parmigiano, finely grated

* Lacinato kale is an Italian variety of kale that's also known as dinosaur kale, Tuscan kale, black kale, and cavolo nero. It has long, slim, dark green leaves and a less bitter, more delicate flavor than curly kale.

** These southern Italian chilies, sold by the jar, are almost as salty as they are spicy, so taste anything you're using them in before you add more salt.

*** Prairie Breeze is an aged cheddar that comes from Milton Creamery in Iowa. It has a nuttiness and tang that we love, but you can use any good aged cheddar here.

MILLENNIUM FALCO

tomato, bread crumbs, parmigiano, chili flakes, onion, pork sausage

1 (12-inch) round of pizza dough (pages 32–35)

43 grams (3 tablespoons) sauce (page 46)

A pinch of chili flakes

Half a garlic clove, peeled and very thinly sliced

40 grams (3 tablespoons) toasted bread crumbs (recipe follows)

40 grams (1½ ounces) parmigiano, finely grated

Some good olive oil

3 or 4 basil leaves, torn into pieces

A quarter of a small red onion, thinly sliced

A golf-ball-size piece (about 40 grams/ 1½ ounces) of pork sausage (page 67)

What makes the Millennium—named for its father, Anthony Falco, one of our original pizzaiolos—so good isn't the toppings themselves as much as the way they're put on the pizza. Layering the bread crumbs with the sauce and cheese just the right way gets you this amazing cheesy-tomatoey sauce when it comes out of the oven. It's what made this pizza a keeper.

Preheat the oven to the highest temperature possible. Place a pizza stone or tiles on the middle rack of the oven and let it heat up for 1 hour.

Put the sauce in the center of the dough round and use the back of a spoon to spread it evenly over the pizza, stopping about half an inch from the edge. Scatter the chili flakes and garlic and then the bread crumbs and parmigiano. Give the whole pizza a swirl of olive oil—not too much. (The idea is that in the oven, the bread crumbs meld with the sauce and cheese to make a thick, flavorful super sauce.)

Scatter the basil and the onion on top. Break up the sausage into marble-size bits and scatter them over the pizza. Bake the pizza until the crust is golden brown and bubbly.

toasted bread crumbs

⅓ stale baguette

Some good olive oil

2 garlic cloves, peeled
and smashed

Kosher salt

Freshly ground black
pepper

You'll have more bread crumbs than you need for this pizza. They store well in the freezer and can be tossed with pasta or scattered over salads or roasted vegetables.

Break the bread into 2 pieces and pulse them in a food processor until you have medium-fine crumbs, or put the bread in a sealed plastic bag and smash it with something heavy until you have medium-fine crumbs.

Coat a sauté pan with olive oil and set it over medium heat. Add the garlic cloves, bread crumbs, and a generous amount of salt and pepper and cook, stirring with a flat-edged wooden spatula or shaking the pan, until the bread crumbs are golden brown, 2 to 3 minutes. Remove from the heat and discard the garlic cloves.

One of our early partners was an Italian who had family in Piedmont. Not long after that day at Pepe's, he got word from his parents that a pizzeria in town had gone out of business and was having a fire sale. The pizza oven was ours for five grand. We decided to do this the same way we decided to give a couple of strangers all of the money we had for the keys to a cinderblock bunker full of junk. It never occurred to us that there might be easier ways to get a pizza oven than having one shipped by boat from Italy.

A month passed. We called. Some guy working at a port in Genoa gave us a line about an inspection. A few weeks passed. We called. The same guy said something about a strike. Some more weeks passed. We called. The guy told us that the ship our pizza oven was on had been lost at sea.

Maybe a month later, in late November, the oven arrived. It was big and red and beautiful and it weighed two and a half tons. Relatively, it took almost as long to get it across the street, through the space next door, and into its home at the head of the concrete bunker as it did for it to get from Genoa to Bushwick. But it got there.

THE LUPO

green garlic, pesto, mozzarella, prosciutto cotto

1 (12-inch) round of pizza dough (pages 32–35)

2 stalks spring garlic (white and tender green parts only), finely chopped, or 1 garlic clove, peeled and minced

35 grams (2½ tablespoons) pesto (recipe follows)

80 grams (2¾ ounces) fresh mozzarella (page 47)

30 grams (2 tablespoons) fresh ricotta

45 grams (1½ ounces) prosciutto cotto,* thinly sliced

Freshly ground black pepper

There are dozens of excellent pizzas you could make in a given season: squash blossom in the summer, ramps in the spring, fennel in the fall. But this one—a spring one in our book, but you can get away with replacing the green garlic with a clove of regular—is our favorite. We borrowed the name for it from Carlo's dog.

Preheat the oven to the highest temperature possible. Place a pizza stone or tiles on the middle rack of the oven and let it heat up for 1 hour.

Scatter the garlic over the dough in an even layer. Place spoonfuls of the pesto around the dough and spread them out with the back of the spoon. Break the mozzarella into small pieces and distribute them over the pizza. Follow them with dollops of the ricotta. Tear the prosciutto slices into smaller pieces if they are large, and layer them over the pizza. Bake the pizza until the crust is golden brown and bubbly. Finish it with a couple of grinds of black pepper.

* Prosciutto cotto is just Italian ham; it's a little less salty and more delicately flavored than regular American ham.

pesto

You'll have more than you need for the pizza here; whatever you don't use on the pizza can be tossed with pasta or served as a condiment for grilled meat or fish.

In a food processor or blender, blend the basil, pine nuts, and parmigiano for about 30 seconds, until a paste forms. While continuing to blend, slowly add the olive oil. Add the salt and pepper and check the seasoning. The pesto will keep in the refrigerator for up to a week and a half, or in the freezer for up to 6 months.

MAKES 170 GRAMS (¾ CUP)

2 big handfuls basil
   leaves

30 grams (2 tablespoons)
    pine nuts

30 grams (1 ounce)
    parmigiano, grated

80 grams (⅓ cup plus
    2 tablespoons) good
    olive oil

A big pinch of salt

A couple of grinds of
black pepper

DA KINE

pineapple, pickled jalapeño, prosciutto cotto, ricotta

The Da Kine—a souped-up Hawaiian pizza with the genius addition of pickled jalapeños from a jar—was a classic from the moment it was born. The trick is to go light on the sauce and cheese to keep the crust from getting soggy.

Preheat the oven to the highest temperature possible. Place a pizza stone or tiles on the middle rack of the oven and let it heat up for 1 hour.

Put the sauce in the center of the dough and use the back of a spoon to spread it evenly over the pizza, stopping about half an inch from the edge. Break the mozzarella into pieces and distribute them over the pizza. Layer the pineapple next, and then scatter the jalapeños. Tear the prosciutto slices into smaller pieces if they are large, and layer them over the pizza. Distribute dollops of the ricotta on top. Bake the pizza until the crust is golden brown and bubbly.

MAKES 1 (12-INCH) PIZZA

1 (12-inch) round of pizza dough (pages 32–35)

30 grams (2 tablespoons) sauce (page 46)

75 grams (2½ ounces) fresh mozzarella (page 47)

60 grams (2 ounces) fresh pineapple, sliced in very thin wedges

20 grams (1½ tablespoons) drained jarred pickled jalapeños, coarsely chopped

45 grams (1½ ounces) prosciutto cotto (see note, page 62), thinly sliced

20 grams (1½ tablespoons) fresh ricotta

BANANA HAMMOCK

garlic, béchamel, mozzarella, parmigiano, pork sausage, peperoncini, onion, cilantro

---

MAKES 1 (12-INCH) PIZZA

---

1 (12-inch) round of pizza dough (pages 32–35)

Half a garlic clove, peeled and very thinly sliced

28 grams (2½ tablespoons) béchamel sauce (recipe follows)

60 grams (2 ounces) fresh mozzarella (page 47)

15 grams (½ ounce) red onion, thinly sliced

15 grams (½ ounce) jarred peperoncini, drained and sliced into ¼-inch-thick rings

A golf-ball-size piece (about 40 grams/ 1½ ounces) of pork sausage (recipe follows)

18 grams (½ ounce) parmigiano, finely grated

2 sprigs cilantro, leaves picked and roughly chopped

Peperoncini are like the pickles of the Mediterranean. They're little peppers sold in jars that add sweetness, acidity, and juicy crunch to whatever they're in—in America, usually antipasto plates and subs. Out there as the mix of ingredients here might sound, it ends up tasting like a classic combination.

Preheat the oven to the highest temperature possible. Place a pizza stone or tiles on the middle rack of the oven and let it heat up for 1 hour.

Scatter the garlic over the dough. Place spoonfuls of the béchamel on the dough and spread them out a little with the back of the spoon. Break the mozzarella into pieces and distribute them over the pizza. Scatter the red onion and peperoncini on top. Break up the sausage into marble-size bits and scatter them over the pizza. Scatter the parmigiano on top, and bake the pizza until the crust is golden brown and bubbly. Garnish with the chopped cilantro and serve.

béchamel sauce

You can use the leftovers of this sauce on any sauceless pizza to add moisture, or in baked pastas. It will keep in the refrigerator for up to three days.

Melt the butter in a saucepan over medium-low heat. Whisk in the flour until the mixture looks smooth. Turn the heat up to medium and cook for 5 to 6 minutes, until the mixture turns golden.

In the meantime, heat the milk and bay leaf in a separate saucepan over medium heat until the milk is about to boil.

Add half the hot milk to the flour mixture, whisking constantly until smooth. Turn up the heat and add the remaining milk, whisking constantly until smooth. Bring the mixture to a boil and cook for 10 minutes, stirring constantly. Keep what you need for the pizza at room temperature and use it within the hour; refrigerate the rest.

MAKES ABOUT 460 GRAMS (1½ CUPS)

- 35 grams (2½ table-spoons) unsalted butter
- 9 grams (2 tablespoons) all-purpose flour
- 470 grams (2 cups) whole milk
- 1 bay leaf

pork sausage

We get our ground pork from Heritage Foods, a company that also operates a food-and-booze-driven radio station out of a shipping container in our backyard. We don't use their pork because they're our neighbors—we use it because it's made from heritage-breed pigs like Red Wattles, Berkshires, and Tamworths, which makes it the most flavorful ground pork around. The better the ground pork you use here, the better the sausage. If you're only making a pizza or two, you'll have leftover sausage. Which isn't really a tragedy. We use it on another pizza in this chapter—the Millennium Falco—but you can also use it in pasta or as part of a breakfast spread.

Toast the fennel seeds in a dry pan over medium heat just until they become fragrant, about a minute.

In a small bowl, combine the salt, brown sugar, and fennel seeds. Add the pinch of chili flakes and a few grinds of black pepper, and combine.

In a larger bowl, combine the pork with the dry ingredient mixture. You can do this by hand. Take a small ball of the pork mixture, and in a nonstick pan over medium-high heat, cook it until it's brown all over. Taste it and adjust the seasoning of the pork mixture if necessary. Use at once, or you can refrigerate the uncooked pork sausage for up to a week or freeze it for up to 2 months.

MAKES 454 GRAMS (1 POUND)

- 4 grams (scant 1 teaspoon) fennel seeds
- 6 grams (2 teaspoons) kosher salt
- 5 grams (1 teaspoon) light brown sugar
- A pinch of chili flakes
- Freshly ground black pepper
- 454 grams (1 pound) ground pork

We arrived in the northern Italian town of Fossano early on a summer afternoon, a journey we'd made because we were about to open a pizzeria and—small detail—we'd never actually made pizza before. Our friend picked us up from the airport and drove us south to the town of Bra, where we stopped off for a bottle of Arneis and some small plates. Four hours later, the girl working our table couldn't keep up with the empty bottles—including half a liter of grappa. Somehow, over some invisible bridge, we got from there to the middle of the night at a club filled with locals. We don't know how or when we got back to where we were staying.

The next memory we have is of a crazy dude who looks like Mel Gibson yelling at us in Italian. Something about how could we show up to work at his place looking and smelling like we did. The good thing was that unless someone was translating, we didn't know what he was saying. We just tried to stay out of the bathroom long enough to watch him demonstrate how to make pizza.

Once we started cooking, we felt a little better. And by the time the fifty or so people we were cooking for got there, we were killing it. There wasn't a person in the room under the age of sixty—cops, town officials, a couple of tour bus drivers. Everybody was congratulating us and telling us how happy they were that we were there.

The pizza was good, but we knew it wasn't going to be our style. Piedmontese pies are like the bread in northern Italy—dry, airy, cracker-crispy. We wanted something with more body, and more salt. What we really learned on that trip was this: We could churn out good pizza for a crowd and make people happy, all while feeling like we wanted to die.

SPECKENWOLF

mozzarella, oregano, onion, mushroom, speck

The Speckenwolf almost never leaves the menu. It's just some tender mushrooms, little piles of speck—a cured ham from northern Italy with a delicate spice and herb flavor—and mozzarella, but for some reason it has a hold on people. Us included.

Preheat the oven to the highest temperature possible. Place a pizza stone or tiles on the middle rack of the oven and let it heat up for 1 hour.

Lightly coat a large sauté pan with olive oil and set it over almost high heat. Add the mushrooms and a pinch of kosher salt, and cook until the mushrooms soften slightly, a few minutes. Remove from the heat and set aside.

Scatter the dried oregano over the dough. Break the mozzarella into pieces and distribute them over the pizza. Layer the mushrooms on top of the mozzarella. Tear each speck slice into two pieces and put each piece in a small heap on the pizza. Scatter the red onion and a pinch of sea salt on top. Bake the pizza until the crust is golden brown and bubbly. Give it two grinds of black pepper, and serve.

MAKES 1 (12-INCH) PIZZA

- 1 (12-inch) round of pizza dough (pages 32–35)

- Some good olive oil

- A small handful of cremini mushrooms

- Kosher salt

- A generous pinch of dried oregano

- 80 grams (2¾ ounces) fresh mozzarella (page 47)

- 3 paper-thin slices of speck

- 15 grams (½ ounce) red onion, thinly sliced

- Sea salt, preferably Maldon

- Freshly ground black pepper

THE WHITE & GREEN
mozzarella, parmigiano, greens

MAKES 1 (12-INCH) PIZZA

1 (12-inch) round of
pizza dough (pages
32–35)

2 handfuls mixed
baby greens, such
as arugula, mustard
greens, and/or chard

Some good olive oil

Half a lemon

Kosher salt

80 grams (2¾ ounces)
fresh mozzarella
(page 47)

18 grams (½ ounce)
parmigiano, finely
grated

Everybody loves the White & Green. It's a simple pizza—a pile of greens on a white pie—that's almost always in the lineup, but it has evolved over the years. Early on, we used baby arugula. Later, when we began growing our own greens, and even later, when we started getting amazing baby greens from the Brooklyn Grange, a rooftop farm in Queens that we helped co-found, we mixed it up. You can use any young greens here. Don't be afraid to be generous with them.

Preheat the oven to the highest temperature possible. Place a pizza stone or tiles on the middle rack of the oven and let it heat up for 1 hour.

In a bowl, lightly dress the greens with a splash of olive oil, a squeeze of lemon, and a pinch of salt.

Crumble the mozzarella into marble-size bits and distribute them over the dough. Drizzle with a splash of olive oil and scatter a pinch of salt and the parmigiano on top. Bake the pizza until the crust is golden brown and bubbly. Put the dressed greens on top and serve.

IN VOLTO

tomato, mozzarella, ricotta, soppressata, roasted red pepper, garlic, basil, oregano

Calzones are trickier than they look. We replaced our calzone with the In Volto—a sort of loose interpretation of a stromboli—during dinner for a while because it was easier for the slammed pizza kitchen to handle. It stayed because everyone loves it so much.

Preheat the oven to the highest temperature possible. Place a pizza stone or tiles on the middle rack of the oven and let it heat up for 1 hour.

Picture the round of dough divided into four vertical sections. Put the sauce in the center of the two middle sections and use the back of a spoon to spread it over the two sections in an even layer. Scatter the garlic, oregano, and basil over the sauce. Break the mozzarella into big chunks and distribute them over the topped area. Distribute spoonfuls of the ricotta on top of that. Scatter the soppressata and roasted red pepper on top.

Fold the edges of the dough over the topped area just until they meet, and pinch them to seal them together. Bake until the crust is golden brown and bubbly.

* Don't create a crust around the edge of the dough round for the In Volto. The dough round should be uniform in thickness, a little more than ⅛ inch, and a little smaller than it would be for a pizza—10 to 11 inches across.

** Soppressata is a hard salami from southern Italy that you can usually get either sweet or spicy. You can find it at Italian markets and at the meat counter in good grocery stores. Ask for the spicy kind and have them slice it for you.

MAKES 1 (10- TO 11-INCH) IN VOLTO

---

1 (10- to 11-inch) round of pizza dough* (pages 32–35)

60 grams (4 generous tablespoons) sauce (page 46)

Half a garlic clove, peeled and very thinly sliced

A pinch of dried oregano

5 or 6 basil leaves, torn into pieces

45 grams (1¾ ounces) fresh mozzarella (page 47)

40 grams (3 tablespoons) fresh ricotta

20 grams (¾ ounce) spicy soppressata,** cut into 6 to 8 (¼-inch-thick) slices

20 grams (¾ ounce) jarred roasted red pepper, drained and sliced into ¼-inch-thick strips

Things are always rosier in hindsight. It's hard to look back fondly on being out of our minds with exhaustion, spending most nights on the floor of a mid-construction kitchen, and getting raped (in the wallet) by a Serbian plumber. But that summer we spent building Roberta's was a sweet one. We were free. Money aside, we could do whatever we wanted to do, whenever we wanted to do it. Even when it sucked as much as it could possibly suck, it was exciting and it was alive and it was ours. And it was really hard to imagine it ever becoming a grind.

By the end of December 2007, there was no money left and no money on the horizon. Rent was late. We didn't have any choice but to open the restaurant. So we put word out to some friends and family, as many as we could. We didn't tell anyone that we didn't have gas or heat yet. We had pizza coming out of our wood-fired oven and we figured, with enough booze, no one would mind. None of us can remember what we were expecting to happen, but what actually happened is that something like four hundred people showed up that night—one of the coldest nights in an already frigid early January. We ran out of pizza at some too early hour and beer not long after that. But people stayed. Other people showed up and brought more to drink. People stayed longer. We figured we were onto something. We may not have had the fundamentals people recognize as essential to a legitimate restaurant: A hostess. A liquor license. A stove. Gas. But we already had the one thing a restaurant can't survive without.

VEGETABLES

There is a lot to be said, and people say it all the time, for treating really nice vegetables simply. But we would argue that vegetables, especially really nice ones, are as worthy a main ingredient as meat or fish. It's pretty rewarding to treat them that way. So while it's true that produce in its prime—in season, in perfect condition—needs very little, it's not a crime to apply more flavors to it than salt and olive oil. What you'll end up with is something much more exciting and much more satisfying than anything that has ever been called a vegetable "side." The recipes that follow all serve two generously. They are not categorized as sides or starters or accompaniments to heartier meals. Eat them however you like.

ROMAINE
candied walnuts, pecorino

SERVES 2
---

2 romaine hearts, ends trimmed, leaves separated

60 to 90 grams (⅓ to ½ cup) roasted garlic dressing (recipe follows)

60 grams (2 ounces) Pecorino Romano

A handful of candied walnuts (recipe follows)

Freshly ground black pepper

This is a seemingly straightforward plate of lettuce that's actually not so straightforward. Some of the garlic for the dressing is roasted, and the nuts require some time and energy, too. But it will all be worth it. The dressing is something like a Caesar but brighter and tangier, and it's insanely good all mixed up with the sweet walnuts and salty cheese. Which is why this salad never leaves the menu. And once you've made the nuts, you'll have them for a nice accompaniment to cheese, or just a good way to ruin your appetite for dinner.

Wash and dry the romaine leaves and put them in a very large bowl—the bigger the better. Pour half the roasted garlic dressing over the leaves, and using your hands, gently scoop the lettuce from the bottom of the bowl up the sides. (We don't recommend using tongs to dress this salad—or any salad. You'll damage the leaves and you won't distribute the dressing evenly.) Gently toss until the leaves are well coated, adding more dressing if needed.

Divide the lettuce between two plates, and using a hand-held fine grater, grate the Pecorino over each plate. Scatter the walnuts over the two plates and give each a grind of black pepper. Serve.

roasted garlic dressing

You'll have more dressing than you need for this recipe. Besides romaine hearts, it works well with any big-leafed, sturdy lettuce, like Bibb.

MAKES 180 GRAMS (1 CUP)

1 head of garlic

175 grams (¾ cup plus 1 tablespoon) good olive oil, plus a splash for the garlic

1 garlic clove, peeled

10 grams (2 teaspoons) Dijon mustard

21 grams (1½ tablespoons) white wine vinegar

28 grams (2 tablespoons) sherry vinegar

2 large egg yolks

5 anchovy fillets

Juice of half a lemon, plus more if needed

Kosher salt

Freshly ground black pepper

Preheat the oven to 350°F. Cut a quarter inch off the head of garlic and place the head, cut side up, on a big square of aluminum foil. Give it a splash of water and a splash of olive oil. Bring the corners of the foil up over the garlic to make a loosely wrapped little package. Bake for a little less than 1 hour. Remove the garlic from the oven and let it cool in the foil. Squeeze the roasted garlic out of 4 or 5 cloves and set the rest aside for another use (it's really good just spread on grilled bread).

Put the roasted garlic, the raw clove of garlic, mustard, vinegars, egg yolks, anchovies, and lemon juice into a blender or food processor and blend for 30 seconds or until combined.

While blending, add the olive oil in a slow, steady stream until it's incorporated and the dressing looks smooth. Taste and add salt, pepper, and more lemon juice as desired. The dressing will keep for a week in the refrigerator.

candied walnuts

Preheat the oven to 350°F. Put the nuts on a baking sheet and when the oven is at temperature, put them in. Roast for 4 minutes and then turn the sheet 180 degrees and roast for another 4 minutes. Remove them from the oven and let them cool. Turn the oven down to 275°F.

In a large bowl, whisk the egg whites until they begin to have body but not until they form soft peaks. Add the brown sugar, honey, and about 10 turns of a pepper grinder's worth of black pepper to the whites, and combine.

Add the walnuts to the mixture and mix with a wooden spoon until they're all well coated. Spread them on a foil-lined baking sheet and sprinkle them evenly with the salt. Put them in the oven and bake for about 12 minutes. Then turn the baking sheet and bake for another 12 minutes; the nuts should be dry, not sticky. Remove them from the oven and let them cool. They'll stay fresh for up to 2 weeks in a sealed container in a cool, dry place.

MAKES 180 GRAMS
(2 CUPS)

---

180 grams (2 cups) walnut halves

2 large (not extra-large or jumbo) egg whites

30 grams (3 packed tablespoons) dark brown sugar

75 grams (¼ cup) honey

Freshly ground black pepper

5 grams (1 teaspoon) kosher salt

For a while, everything was perfect. The tables were full until closing most nights. The pizza was good. We were running the floor from in front of the oven and it was working. We had two of the best servers we've ever known giving generously of good old-fashioned hospitality. If you came to the restaurant in those early days, your night probably went something like this: You came, presumably wearing a coat, since it was almost always below freezing at night that winter and we didn't have heat. You brought wine or a couple of six-packs. If you'd been before, you probably also brought a little whiskey to get you through the latter end of the evening. You ordered some pizza and the salad. There was one. And maybe you had some cured meat that Carlo had made in his dad's basement on Long Island to start. Or if the back kitchen was feeling creative, some cannellini beans slow-cooked in beer and spooned over toast. You kept your coat on and you fiddled with the knobs on the stupid space heaters positioned around the room that made god-awful sounds every time someone got too close to them. You drank a lot. You shared what you were drinking with the pizza kitchen guys. They probably shared a joint back. You ate. You hung out until late. You went home happy. That's pretty much how it went in those days. It was awesome. We really wanted it to stay that way.

HEN OF THE WOODS
thyme, olive oil, salt

In the early days of limited resources and equipment, we spent a lot of time trying to figure out not just what would work, but what we could do really well. This is a simple dish—perfect if you do it right. They serve a version of it at a little counter-seat restaurant in the Boqueria, the big market in Barcelona. If you can't get wild hen of the woods, cultivated ones—or oyster or king trumpet mushrooms—will work too.

Coat the bottom of a large sauté pan with olive oil and place it over almost high heat. When the oil is hot, add the mushrooms and a pinch of kosher salt. Let the mushrooms start to caramelize, 3 to 4 minutes, and then flip them individually. After another few minutes, add the butter, toss to coat, and remove the pan from the heat. Add a good splash of sherry vinegar, the thyme leaves, and big pinch of sea salt. Serve.

SERVES 2

Some good olive oil

250 grams (about 9 ounces) hen of the woods mushrooms, trimmed and cleaned

Kosher salt

30 grams (2 tablespoons) salted butter

Sherry vinegar

2 sprigs thyme, leaves picked

Sea salt, preferably Maldon

MINER'S LETTUCE
sorrel vinaigrette, bottarga

4 big handfuls miner's lettuce, washed

Kosher salt

Freshly ground black pepper

Some good olive oil

90 grams (½ cup) sorrel vinaigrette (recipe follows)

10 grams (about ⅓ ounce) bottarga*

We only learned when attempting to explain what miner's lettuce is for the purposes of this book that it is so called because it's incredibly rich in vitamin C, and that during the mid-1800s gold rush, prospectors used to eat it to stave off scurvy. Interesting fact! What we already knew about miner's lettuce is that it grows like wildfire on the West Coast beginning in March and that it has a nutty, vegetal flavor and a meaty bite that makes for an awesome salad. It's not native to the East Coast but you can grow it here, and we do, in the garden at the restaurant. Miner's lettuce is good mixed with other greens and as a garnish for all kinds of things but it's at its best solo, as it is here with a green vinaigrette to echo its springiness and a salty, complex hit of bottarga.

Put the miner's lettuce in a big bowl, season it with a little salt and pepper, and dress it very lightly with olive oil, tossing it gently with your hands.

Divide the lettuce between two wide, shallow bowls and use a squeeze bottle or a spoon to drop the sorrel vinaigrette in a few places in among the leaves in each bowl. Using a hand-held fine grater, shave the bottarga over each bowl. Serve.

* Bottarga is cured fish roe—usually from tuna or mullet—that is a kitchen staple in Sicily and Sardinia. It has a briny, almost buttery flavor that's not really comparable to anything else. It's not cheap, but you'll only use a little bit of it, no matter what you're making (see sources, page 282). Wrap it up tightly after you use it and store it in the freezer. It will keep for a few months, at which point the flavor will start to lose its punch.

sorrel vinaigrette

This recipe calls for a juicer. A few other recipes in these pages do too, not to be annoying and chef-y, but because the juice of a fresh fruit or vegetable can do a lot for a dish made with that fruit or vegetable. In this case, for instance, if you just blend all the sorrel with olive oil for the vinaigrette, you'll lose a good amount of intense, lemony sorrel flavor. If you mix in pure sorrel juice with the pureed sorrel, you recapture that intense flavor. If you don't have a juicer, you can blanch and puree all of the sorrel rather than juicing some of it. The vinaigrette just won't be as concentrated and bright. Either way, you can use the leftovers for salads made with delicate greens or herbs, or drizzle it over grilled fish.

Prepare a pot of very well salted boiling water and a big bowl of ice water. Have ready a chilled container for the juiced sorrel.

Blanch 2 bunches of the sorrel in the boiling water for no more than 30 seconds, and then plunge them into the bowl of ice water. Drain the sorrel and put it in a blender with a big splash of olive oil, and blend for about 20 seconds. Transfer it to a mixing bowl.

Put the other bunch of sorrel into a juicer and juice it into the chilled container (otherwise it will turn from green to brown). Add the sorrel juice to the pureed sorrel with another small splash of olive oil, whisk together, and taste. Continue to add olive oil a drizzle at a time until you have a good balance. (You want the olive oil to temper the intensity of the sorrel but not to drown it.) Add a big squeeze of lemon juice and season with salt and pepper to taste. The vinaigrette will keep in the refrigerator for up to a week.

* Sorrel is a plant with slender, arrow-shaped leaves and a potent lemony flavor. A member of the rhubarb family, it's in season from mid-spring through the end of summer. The varieties you're likely to come across at the farmers' market are French and English. Look for bright green sorrel with stems that are supple, not woody.

MAKES 135 GRAMS (¾ CUP)

---

3 bunches sorrel,* ends trimmed

Some good olive oil

Half a lemon

Kosher salt

Freshly ground black pepper

ASPARAGUS

egg yolk, trout roe, lemon

SERVES 2

---

225 grams (about 1 cup)
sake

Rice vinegar

Half a lemon

Some good olive oil

35 grams (2½ table-
spoons) wild trout roe*

16 or so medium-thin
asparagus stalks

Kosher salt

Freshly ground black
pepper

2 large egg yolks

Sea salt, preferably
Maldon

* Trout roe—one of many
domestic fish roes that people
like to call American caviar—is
a nice bright orange color. It
has a clean, very lightly sweet
flavor. People make a thing out
of steelhead trout roe, but any
wild trout roe is good.

It's amazing how you can start to take things for granted. On the East Coast, where the asparagus season is short—later-starting and shorter than a lot of restaurant menus would lead you to believe—its arrival used to be a very big deal. Now that there's more and more interesting spring produce available at the farmers' market, asparagus is beginning to seem a little mundane. If you feel that way about asparagus, this dish will cure you. And even if you don't, it will make you happy.

A day before you want to eat this dish, marinate the trout roe. You're doing this for two reasons: One, trout roe can be tough, and marinating it will soften it. Two, the infusion from the sake gives the roe a deeper, more complex flavor. Use sake you'd be happy to drink.

In a small saucepan, bring the sake to a boil and let it go for about a minute; then remove it from the heat and let it cool. Add a small splash of rice vinegar, the grated zest from the lemon half (save the lemon half—you'll need it later), and a splash of olive oil, and transfer the mixture to a glass or plastic container that you can seal. Put the trout roe in the container, cover it, and leave it in the refrigerator for at least 8 hours and no more than 12.

When you're ready to cook the asparagus, take off the woody ends of the stalks—just bend the stalks near the base and they'll break in a natural place. Rinse, dry, and season them with kosher salt and pepper. Put a large sauté pan over almost high heat and add a couple of splashes of olive oil. Throw the asparagus in the pan and let it cook, turning it once or twice, until it's no longer crunchy but still has a bite. This should take 5 or 6 minutes, depending on the thickness of the asparagus. To test the doneness, pick up a stalk after 4 minutes or so, let it cool for

a few seconds, and hold it horizontally. If it doesn't bow at all, it's not done yet. If it bows a little, it's done. (If it bows a lot, it's overdone.) Transfer the asparagus to a plate lined with paper towels.

Divide the asparagus between two plates and put a spoonful of trout roe, including a little of the marinade liquid, on top of it.

Fill a small saucepan almost to the top with water and place it over high heat. When the water is almost boiling, remove the pan from the heat. Put an egg yolk on a perforated spoon and dunk it quickly in the hot water. Do this three or four times, and then place the warm yolk on top of the asparagus, near the roe. Repeat with the other egg yolk. The yolks will look raw but they'll be warm all the way through.

Squeeze a little lemon juice over both plates. Drizzle with a little olive oil, and sprinkle with sea salt and black pepper. Serve right away.

CORN

'nduja, purple basil

SERVES 2

2 ears of corn

A spoonful of 'nduja*

Some good olive oil

Kosher salt

A handful of purple basil, small leaves only (Thai basil or mint will work too)

* 'Nduja is a spicy, fatty, spreadable sausage from the Calabria region of Italy. We used to have to smuggle it in from Florence, but now you can get it in the United States.

When corn is in peak season, it's so good you don't even have to cook it. You *shouldn't* cook it. See if the vendor at the farmers' market will take a buck to let you bite into an ear before you buy more. You want the sweetest, crunchiest corn you can get. If you've got perfect corn—like if you're happy eating it right off the cob—what follows isn't so much a recipe as instructions for how to plate.

Take the kernels off the corn. To do this, a lot of people stand the corn up in a bowl (to catch flying kernels) and run a sharp knife down it from top to bottom. But it's actually easier if you just lay the corn flat on a surface and shave the kernels off with the knife.

If the corn tastes absolutely perfect to you as is, skip the next step. Otherwise, cook the kernels in a very hot dry pan, giving the pan an occasional shake, for a minute or two—just until they give off a roasted corn smell, not until they start to color.

Take a generous spoonful of 'nduja and spread it across two plates; you're going for a wide band that arcs across the plate, so that you get a little 'nduja with each bite of corn. Dress the corn with a little olive oil, a tiny pinch of salt, and the purple basil leaves. Garnish with a little more olive oil, and serve.

SNAP PEAS
smoked ricotta, pickled rhubarb, anchovy bread crumbs

SERVES 2

300 grams (10½ ounces) snap peas, bright green and heavy for their size, washed and patted dry

Some good olive oil

Kosher salt

White balsamic vinegar

50 grams (about ¼ cup) Salvatore Bklyn smoked ricotta,* at room temperature

30 grams (about 3 table-spoons) pickled rhubarb (recipe follows)

A handful of parsley, leaves picked

15 grams (¼ cup) anchovy bread crumbs (recipe follows)

Everybody tries to capture spring on a plate. Understandable, as the season and its vegetables don't hang around for very long. So come that time of year, young lettuces, baby vegetables, and grilled aspara-gus are everywhere. Those are good but this dish is springier than all of those things. It's also hearty. There's smoky ricotta to balance the sweet peas, tart rhubarb, and salty, crunchy anchovy bread crumbs. Plus, as spring vegetables go, snap peas are up there. They're a neon sign that spring is slipping into the rear view and summer's almost here.

Peel the strings off all of the snap peas. Put a large sauté pan over high heat and coat it with olive oil. When the olive oil is really hot, throw in the snap peas. Leave them alone for about 30 seconds, and then give the pan a couple of good shakes and cook for another 30 seconds. You want them to start to blacken in places. Remove the pan from the heat and salt the snap peas. Transfer them to a bowl and sprinkle them with a little white balsamic, a drizzle of olive oil, and a little more salt.

Place small spoonfuls of the ricotta in a few places on two plates. Divide the snap peas between the plates and put a few very small spoonfuls of rhubarb on each plate, in among the peas. Scatter a few parsley leaves and the bread crumbs on top. Serve.

* How obnoxious to specify a small-batch ingredient made in Brooklyn! But Salvatore Bklyn makes incredible, very spreadable smoked ricotta, and the truth is that it's part of what makes this dish so good. If you can't find it, substitute any soft smoked fresh ricotta. If it's not very spoonable, loosen it up with a little whole milk. If you can't find smoked fresh ricotta at all, use the highest quality fresh ricotta you can find, mascarpone, or a nice soft goat cheese. The results will still be good.

pickled rhubarb

Unlike some other pickling you may have done, this process doesn't require heat. That's the good news. The possibly bad news is that, at least at the restaurant, it requires a vacuum-sealing machine (we use the Cryovac brand). These machines suck the air out of packages and vacuum-seal them, allowing for faster marinating of meats, quick pickling, and many other really useful things. The reason for using one here is that it allows for cold pickling, which preserves the flavor of the rhubarb. Submerging rhubarb in hot water dulls the flavor. More good news, though, is that you can do a slightly less efficient home version of vacuum sealing that will work just fine. You'll have more pickled rhubarb than you need for the snap peas; it's really good on raw and grilled fish. And vanilla ice cream.

In a container, combine the sugar with the vinegar, give it a stir, and let the sugar dissolve.

Using a peeler, remove the tough, stringy outer layer of the rhubarb. Then cut it in a very small dice, about ¼ inch.

Fill a big pot with water. Put the rhubarb and the pickling liquid in a gallon-size zipper-lock bag; don't seal it up. Lower the bag very, very slowly into the pot of water until you reach the top of the bag. While the bag is still in the water, seal it tightly and then remove it from the pot. Refrigerate the bag for at least 12 hours before using the rhubarb. Whatever you don't use for this dish can be stored in the pickling liquid in a container in the refrigerator for up to 2 weeks.

MAKES 120 GRAMS (ABOUT 1 CUP)

30 grams (scant ¼ cup) sugar

310 grams (1½ cups) rice vinegar

200 grams (7 ounces) rhubarb (about 2 large stalks)

anchovy bread crumbs

MAKES 100 GRAMS (ABOUT 1 CUP)

A very stale baguette

Some good olive oil

4 or 5 anchovy fillets, finely chopped

Grated zest of half a lemon

Kosher salt

Freshly ground black pepper

You'll have more bread crumbs than you need for this dish. They store well in the freezer for up to a month and can be tossed with pasta or scattered over salads or roasted vegetables.

Preheat the oven to 350°F. Break the bread into chunks and either put them in a zipper-lock bag and smash them with a rolling pin or put them in a food processor and pulse it for a minute or two. You want the bread crumbs to be coarse—a little bigger than peas.

In a bowl, toss the crumbs with a couple of big splashes of olive oil, the anchovies, lemon zest, and a lot of salt and pepper. Spread them out on a baking sheet and bake for about 30 minutes, until golden brown to slightly darker.

SUCRINE
pecorino fiore, dried cherry

Sucrine is a sweet, buttery lettuce—a little like Bibb or Little Gem but sweeter and more buttery. It's not the easiest lettuce to grow, so it can be hard to find. Try, though. Press at your farmers' market and you might find someone trying to grow it or convince someone to start. Raw and barely dressed with olive oil, lemon juice, and salt, sucrine is really good. Cooked as follows, it's awesome alongside grilled chicken or pork or nothing at all.

Coat a large sauté pan with olive oil—not too much—and place it over medium-high heat. When the pan is hot, add the cherries. When they start to swell up, after about 30 seconds or so, throw in the sucrine and add a pinch of salt. You want the lettuce to have a bite, so cook it only until it's warmed through, a couple of minutes at most. Add a splash of sherry vinegar to the pan and transfer the sucrine to four plates. Shave the pecorino over each plate and serve.

SERVES 4

Some good olive oil

45 grams (⅓ cup) dried cherries

4 heads sucrine, outer leaves picked off and discarded, ends trimmed, leaves washed

Kosher salt

Sherry vinegar

40 grams (1½ ounces) Pecorino Fiore Sardo*

* This is a pecorino from Sardinia that's younger and milder than Pecorino Romano.

PURSLANE

goat's milk yogurt, aged gouda, blueberry

SERVES 2

115 grams (½ cup) goat's milk yogurt

Half a lemon

Kosher salt

Freshly ground black pepper

4 big handfuls purslane, trimmed and washed

Some good olive oil

A handful of blueberries or any summer berry

1 watermelon radish* (or 2 or 3 smaller radishes), sliced paper-thin (see note, page 105)

30 grams (1 ounce) roomano pradera**

White balsamic vinegar

* You can find these Chinese radishes at Asian markets, some farmers' markets, and even better supermarkets. They're a little bigger than a golf ball, mild rather than spicy, and an amazing hot pink color inside.

Purslane is a succulent that's abundant around here from late spring through the very end of summer—and by "around here" we mean the East Coast generally and specifically in Brooklyn in the backyard of a woman who grows tons of it. That's where we get ours. It has a refreshing crunch and a clean, lemony taste that works well with all kinds of summer ingredients. The radishes aren't mandatory, but besides adding crunch, they turn the whole thing into a pretty summer plate.

In a bowl, mix the goat's milk yogurt with a big squeeze of lemon juice and season it with salt and pepper. Add another squeeze of lemon juice and taste it. Adjust the acid and seasoning to taste. The brighter and bolder the seasoned yogurt, the better.

In a big bowl, dress the purslane very lightly with a splash of olive oil and a squeeze of lemon juice, and season it with salt and pepper, tossing it gently with your hands.

Divide the purslane between two plates and either put the goat's milk mixture in a squeeze bottle or use a spoon to drop it into the gaps in the purslane. (Tossing the purslane with the yogurt makes a big mess; this way, you can get yogurt with each bite but it doesn't coat the purlsane.)

Place the blueberries in among the purslane. Dress the radish slices with a little lemon juice and salt, and place them in a few spots on each plate. Use a peeler to shave the roomano over each plate. Shake a few drops of white balsamic over each, and serve.

** Roomano pradera is an aged Gouda from Holland, best described as the pecorino of the Netherlands. It's delicious. If you can't find it, use the best aged Gouda you can get.

FAIRY TALE EGGPLANT

mascarpone, black mint

The only way to screw up this dish is to use garden-variety eggplants—
the kind you'd use for eggplant Parmesan. Fairy Tales are much
smaller—just two or three inches long—and have incredibly delicate
flavor and very tender flesh. The secret to this dish at the restaurant is
roasting the eggplant in the wood-fired oven just until it's just starting to
brown at the edges. The smokiness from the fire works magic. But a
quick roast in your own hot oven or a few minutes in a scorching pan
will get you more than close enough.

If you're using an oven to roast the eggplant, preheat it to the highest
temperature possible, ideally 500°F. Slice the eggplants in half lengthwise, dress them with a little olive oil, and season them generously with
salt and pepper. Place them skin side down on a baking sheet and roast
them for about 15 minutes, until they begin to color. Let them cool to
room temperature.

If you're cooking the eggplant on the stovetop, coat a cast-iron pan with
olive oil and put it over almost high heat. Slice the eggplants in half
lengthwise and season them with salt and pepper. Cook on one side for
5 to 7 minutes, then flip and cook the same amount of time on the other
side. (These are little guys; they don't take long. You want them firm,
with a bite, not mushy.) Let the eggplant cool to room temperature.

Spoon the mascarpone onto two plates. Arrange the eggplant on the
plates, drizzle with a little olive oil, and season with a little more salt
and pepper. Scatter the mint leaves over the eggplant and serve.

SERVES 2

---

5 or 6 Fairy Tale eggplants
(or 3 of the smallest
Japanese eggplants
you can find)

Some good olive oil

Kosher salt

Freshly ground black
pepper

30 grams (generous
2½ tablespoons)
mascarpone, at room
temperature

A small handful of
black mint leaves*

* Black mint is a Peruvian
variety with an incredibly pure,
really strong mint flavor. If you
can't find it, use any fresh mint.

CARROT
smoked ricotta, radish, lemon

This is a simple dish. Roast a nice firm bunch of young carrots until they're just beginning to caramelize but they're still orange—or in the case of heirloom carrots, whatever color they were when you put them in the oven. Then throw in spice, smoke, and acid to balance all that sweetness. That's it.

Preheat the oven to 400°F. If you have young, tender heirloom carrots, it's not necessary to peel them. It's up to you. Trim the greens and make sure the ends are clean. Toss the carrots with a little olive oil and salt, and put them on a baking sheet. Roast them for 15 to 20 minutes, giving the pan a shake midway through, until they're just beginning to caramelize at the edges—they should be barely starting to brown. Remove them from the oven, sprinkle with some white balsamic, season with a little salt and pepper, and let them cool for a few minutes.

In the meantime, juice the remaining raw carrot in a juicer. Mix the ricotta with a little bit of olive oil to loosen it up and season it. Spoon the ricotta mixture onto two plates. Divide the carrots between the plates and scatter the sliced radishes over them. Spoon the carrot juice onto the plates. Give just the carrots a squeeze of lemon juice and a drizzle of olive oil. (It might seem fussy but this is a pretty plate and if you just drizzle juice and oil over everything, things will get messy.) Sprinkle with a very little bit of sea salt and serve.

* Slice the radish as thin as you can—ideally on a mandoline, otherwise, with a very sharp knife.

SERVES 2

350 grams (about 12 ounces) young carrots, preferably heirloom

Some good olive oil

Kosher salt

White balsamic vinegar

Freshly ground black pepper

1 large carrot, or 12 grams (1½ tablespoons) store-bought carrot juice

50 grams (about ¼ cup) Salvatore Bklyn smoked ricotta, at room temperature (see note, page 96)

Half a watermelon radish, sliced paper-thin*

Half a lemon

Sea salt, preferably Maldon

BEETS
crème fraîche, bottarga, dill

3 large egg whites

340 grams (1½ cups plus 2 tablespoons) kosher salt, plus more as needed

4 or 5 small beets, or 2 medium to large beets, greens trimmed

½ cup (4 ounces) crème fraîche (recipe follows)

Freshly ground black pepper

A small handful of red watercress, trimmed, or dill, chopped

15 grams (½ ounce) bottarga (see note, page 88)

The trick here is salt-roasting, an age-old method that concentrates flavors and preserves moisture. It does amazing things to beets. Use heirloom beets—which are usually on the smaller side and come in shades of pink, yellow, and orange—if you can get them, but this technique will do wonders for any beet.

Preheat the oven to 350°F. In a bowl, beat the egg whites with a whisk until soft peaks begin to form. Fold the salt into the egg whites. Spread half the salt mixture on the bottom of a small roasting pan or baking dish, and put the beets on top. Spoon the rest of the mixture on top of the beets, making sure they're well covered.

Roast for 1 to 1½ hours, depending on the size of the beets. When you can pierce them easily with a metal skewer or the tip of a sharp knife, they're done. Remove the pan from the oven and let it sit for 10 minutes, at which point the beets should be cool enough to handle. (Don't let them sit longer than that because you want to serve them warm.) Use a knife to crack open the salt crust. Remove the beets and peel them.

Season the crème fraîche with a pinch of salt and a couple of grinds of black pepper. Divide it between two plates, putting a few spoonfuls on each. Break the beets into pieces slightly bigger than bite-size and put them on top of the crème fraîche. Scatter the watercress over the beets, and using a hand-held fine grater, grate the bottarga on top. Serve.

BEETS

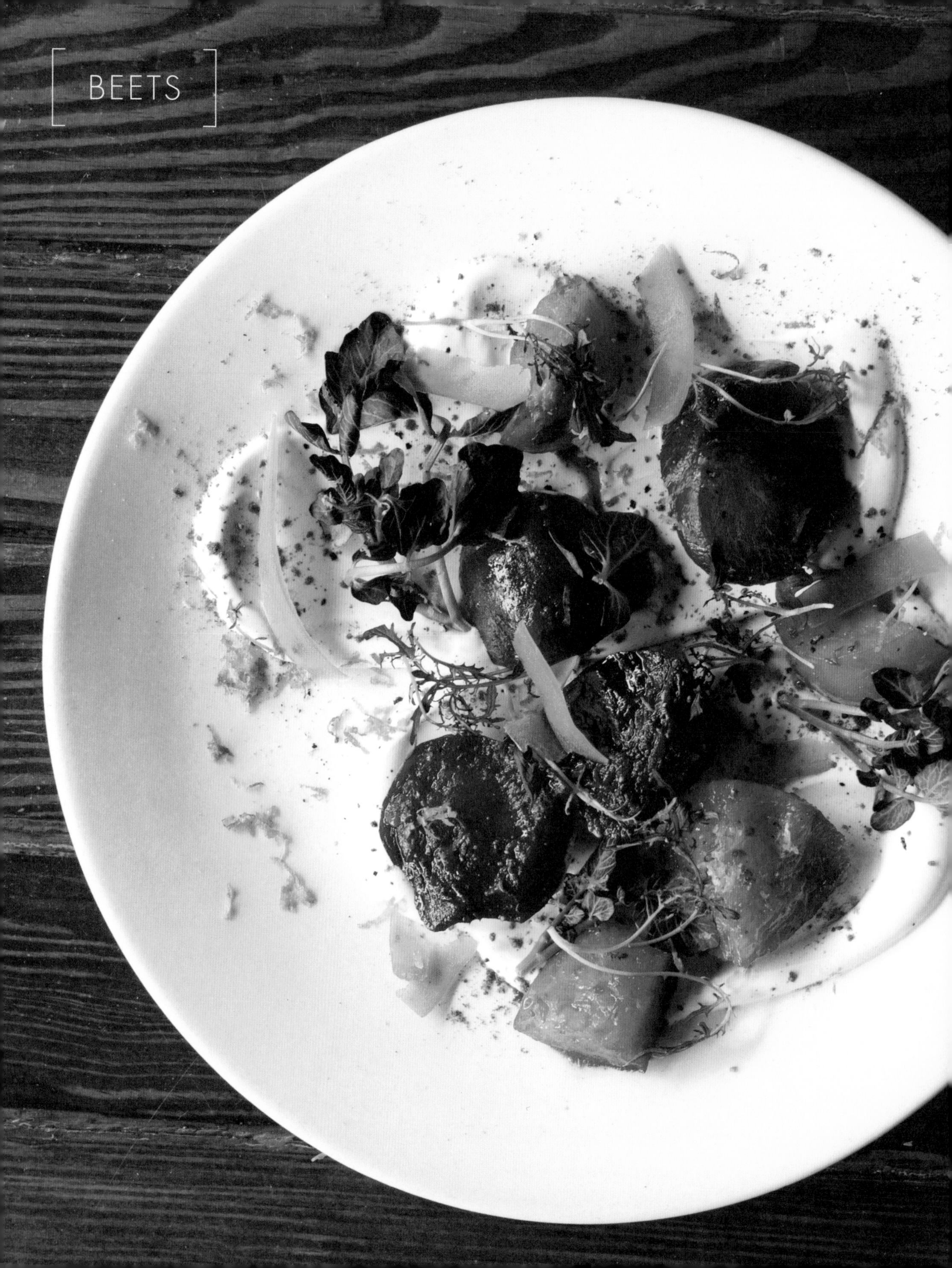

crème fraîche

You can substitute store-bought here, but homemade is so much creamier and fresher tasting, and so easy to make, that we encourage you to try it.

Combine the heavy cream and buttermilk in a nonreactive bowl. Cover the bowl loosely with a kitchen towel and let it sit at room temperature for 24 hours until slightly thickened. Transfer the crème fraîche to a glass container with a lid, seal it, and refrigerate it. It will keep for up to 2 weeks.

MAKES 180 GRAMS
(1 GENEROUS CUP)

240 grams (1 cup) heavy cream (not ultra-pasteurized), at room temperature

20 grams (2 tablespoons) buttermilk, preferably cultured, at room temperature

APPLE
burrata, sorrel, honey

At the restaurant, the process of choosing apples for this dish is intense.
We're pretty sure it's as intense as a Senate confirmation hearing.
As with corn, it's essential that you taste apples before you buy them
at the farmers' market. It will be worth the couple extra bucks. Even
when you know you like a particular variety—Pink Lady, say, or Pacific
Rose—you should still take a bite out of one of the ones you're buying
to make sure they're in perfect condition. For this dish, you want an
extremely crisp, tart but not too tart apple. The combination of a perfect
apple with creamy burrata is so good that if you haven't tried it you
should stop what you're doing and try it right now.

If your apples haven't been in the refrigerator, put them there for at
least half an hour before you move on to the next step.

Cut the apples into 4 big sections each, and core them. Cut those sections up into medium-size chunks; they shouldn't be totally uniform
in shape. Put the apple chunks in a medium bowl and add the burrata,
torn into chunks, some of its liquid, and a pinch of salt, and toss it all
together. You want the apple chunks to be well coated with the cheese
and liquid.

Divide the apples between two plates and give each plate a grind of
black pepper. Drizzle with a little honey and garnish generously with
torn sorrel leaves (the sorrel isn't just for looks—it adds a really nice
lemony flavor). Serve.

SERVES 2

---

2 apples, such as
  Winesap or Pink Lady,
  washed and chilled

100 grams (3½ ounces)
  burrata,* in its liquid

  Kosher salt

  Freshly ground black
  pepper

  Honey, to taste

  A handful of sorrel
  leaves (see note, page
  91), torn

* Burrata is an Italian cheese,
originally from Puglia, that's
a relative of mozzarella but
much, much creamier. There
are American versions of it
now too.

TREVISO
gran blu di bufala, vin cotto

SERVES 2

---

1 head Treviso, Tardivo, or radicchio

Some good olive oil

Ayu fish sauce*

Half a lemon

Kosher salt

White balsamic vinegar

50 grams (about 2 ounces) gran blu di bufala (or good Gorgonzola piccante)

Vin cotto or saba**

---

* You're probably familiar with the Vietnamese version of fish sauce, which is salty and delicious. Ayu fish sauce, made from a Japanese freshwater fish, is also salty but a little sweeter and with a deeper flavor. If you have to substitute Vietnamese fish sauce, try Red Boat, which isn't as salty as most.

Treviso has a typically complicated Italian backstory. It's a kind of chicory—a bitter winter green—that has wine-colored leaves with big white veins running through them. *Radicchio rosso* is the general term for chicories with wine-colored leaves that have big white veins running through them, and within that category there are many different varieties. The best is Treviso, which can technically be called that—because the Italians like to be that way—only if it is actually from Treviso, the town in the northeast corner of Italy where it originated. As relates to the small, round radicchio you've seen in supermarkets, Treviso has longer, slimmer leaves and a deeper flavor.

It's almost impossible to get true Treviso. But you might be able to find Tardivo, a very closely related variety that's also long, slim, and flavorful, at good produce markets or farmers' markets in the fall and winter. That's what we use (and we call it Treviso on the menu because it basically is, and because Treviso is a more recognizable word than Tardivo). If all you can get your hands on is supermaket radicchio, this dish is still worth making. Treviso and its relatives are cooking lettuces. Hit with the right amount of heat, their bitterness softens and they start to taste like meat.

Peel away the outer leaves of the Treviso and trim an inch from the bottom. Separate all the leaves. Put the leaves in a bowl and toss them gently with a splash of olive oil, a smaller splash of ayu, a squeeze of lemon juice, and a pinch of salt (not too much—the ayu is salty).

Put a splash of olive oil in a large nonstick sauté pan and place it over medium-high heat. When the oil is shimmering, throw in the Treviso. Let it wilt for 2 to 3 minutes, giving the pan an occasional shake, and add a splash of balsamic.

Arrange the Treviso on two plates and crumble the gran blu over it. Finish with a drizzle of vin cotto and a squeeze of lemon juice per plate, and serve.

** Vin cotto is a dark, sweet, syrupy Italian condiment made from unfermented grape juice. If you can't find it, you can substitute saba, a grape must reduction that's essentially the same thing.

CABBAGE
apple, turnip, bonito

Cabbage is underrated. For this dish, meaty Savoy gets blanched for a few seconds, so that it's tender but still has a bite, and then bathed in bonito butter. Crunchy napa, the stuff kimchi is made with, is dressed with a mix of acid and heat, from a Japanese spice. A little turnip and apple go in for sweetness. The result will floor anyone who usually isn't all that into cabbage.

Cut the bok choy into 1- to 1½-inch pieces. Cut the apple into ½-inch chunks. In a large bowl, dress the bok choy, apple, and napa cabbage with the togarashi dressing. Set aside.

Tear the Savoy cabbage into pieces a little bigger than bite-size. In a large sauté pan over medium-low heat, warm the Savoy with three-quarters of the bonito butter, tossing it gently to coat. Transfer it to the bowl containing the apple.

Warm the remaining bonito butter in the same sauté pan until just melted.

In the meantime, use your hands to gently toss the napa mixture together. Give the mixture a squeeze of lemon juice and a pinch of salt, and briefly toss. Check the seasoning and adjust if necessary.

Divide the cabbage mixture between two plates and drizzle the melted bonito butter on top. Garnish each plate with a few slices of turnip and the grated horseradish, and serve.

* Blanch the bok choy and Savoy cabbage in a big pot—together is fine—of well-salted boiling water for 10 to 15 seconds. Each should turn a little brighter green and retain a good bite.

SERVES 2

21 grams (¾ ounce) blanched* bok choy (from about a quarter of a head, trimmed)

Half a Granny Smith apple

40 grams (2 to 3 leaves) napa and/or purple cabbage, torn (generous ½ cup)

Togarashi dressing (recipe follows)

90 grams (3 to 4 leaves) blanched* Savoy cabbage (1 generous cup)

60 grams (4 tablespoons) bonito butter (recipe follows)

Half a lemon

Kosher salt

Half a Tokyo turnip, shaved paper-thin (see note, page 105)

2 grams (1 scant tablespoon) grated fresh horseradish

togarashi dressing

MAKES 46 GRAMS
(¼ CUP)

5 grams (2½ teaspoons) shichimi togarashi*

20 grams (2 tablespoons) ayu fish sauce (see note, page 112)

22 grams (1½ table-spoons) rice vinegar

4 grams (1 teaspoon) red wine vinegar

A pinch of kosher salt

You won't have leftovers of this, but make it again to dress sautéed greens, raw vegetables, or slaws. It has good acidity and a little kick.

In a bowl, whisk together all the ingredients. If not using immediately, cover and refrigerate for up to a week.

* Also called seven-spice powder, shichimi togarashi is a Japanese spice made from ground chilies, Sichuan peppercorns, dried orange peel, dried ginger, dried seaweed, and sesame seeds. It has a nice strong heat that doesn't linger.

bonito butter

MAKES 115 GRAMS
(8 TABLESPOONS)

42 grams (5 tablespoons) water, at room temperature

115 grams (8 tablespoons) salted butter, at room temperature

3 grams (⅓ cup) bonito flakes (see note, page 121)

Any time you make a compound butter, it's worth making more than you need. This is a rich, earthy one that's a great last-minute addition to seafood risotto, pasta, or vegetables, such as asparagus and green beans, served warm. It will keep in the refrigerator for up to a week and in the freezer for up to a month.

In a bowl, mix all of the ingredients together until well combined. If not using immediately, form into a rough cylinder, wrap in plastic wrap, and refrigerate.

It sounds dramatic to say that a newspaper review changed everything, but that's what happened. Three months after we opened, the *New York Times* published a review of Roberta's by Peter Meehan in their $25 and Under column. It was a positive review, but we didn't brace ourselves for much. It was hard to picture anyone who lived in Manhattan putting down their newspaper and rustling up a group of friends to come to Bushwick. We thought maybe we'd get some more people from Williamsburg and some people willing to ride a few stops farther on the L from the East Village. What we got ultimately changed our clientele for good. And because it changed our clientele it changed our business and the way we ran it.

You can pretend that you can get loaded behind the pizza counter and that people will get loaded with you and life will go on with you running your business the way you live your life and everyone will be happy. Maybe it could. But not once you get discovered. Not once you get successful by most people's definition instead of just your own. The first blazer and tie that crossed the threshold, we knew everything was going to have to change.

DEAD MAN WALK-IN

STONE COLD STEVE WALK-IN 3:16

CHRISTOPHER WALK-IN

WALK-IN PHOENIX

WALK-IN TEXAS RANGER

The "Walk in" Dead

THESE BOOTS WERE MADE FOR WALK-IN

LUKE SKY-WALK IN

I Just want a woman
who will take long
Walk-ins on the beach
with me. That's all.

I'm walk-in on sunshine!

WALK-IN TO THE JUNGLE!

"I SAW YOU AND HIM...WALK-IN IN THE RAIN..."

Walk-in like an Egyptian

WALK IN ROLL !

WALK-IN on the MOON

MIL-WALKIN BEST

Keep on Walk-IN The Free World

Piggy Long Walk-IN's

By Appointment Only. No WALK-IN

CELTUCE
kumquat, bonito, goat's milk

Celtuce is a Chinese vegetable that has an addictive cucumber-like crunch and a grassy, celery-like flavor. You can find it at good Asian produce markets almost any time of year. Look for a long, thick stem with a bunch of lettuce-like leaves at the top. (You'll be discarding the leaves and keeping the stem.) Goat's milk has mild sweetness and subtle tang that make a nice backdrop for the flavors here.

Toast the Marconas in a dry sauté pan over medium heat for a minute or two, until they're just starting to color. Let them cool and then chop them coarsely.

Prepare an ice bath. Using a peeler, remove the tough outside layer of the celtuce, and then cut it in irregular shapes—crosswise for cylinders, lengthwise for planks, for example. Transfer the pieces to the ice water as you go to keep the celtuce from browning.

Add a splash of olive oil to the goat's milk and season it with salt and pepper. Thinly slice each kumquat crosswise so that you end up with thin rounds. Drain the celtuce and pat it dry, and then dress it with a good splash of olive oil, a splash of white balsamic, and salt and pepper.

Divide the goat's milk between two wide shallow bowls. Arrange the celtuce pieces on top and place the kumquat slices randomly on each serving. Add fingerfuls of the chopped Marconas in a few spots, and scatter the bonito flakes over the top. Serve.

** Bonito flakes are a staple of Japanese cooking made from dried smoked fish; they're used to make dashi and many, many other things. The whole flakes are papery and delicate, and here they add nice texture and a little brininess.

SERVES 2

75 grams (½ cup) raw Marcona almonds

1 celtuce, stalk only

Some good olive oil

115 grams (½ cup) goat's milk

Kosher salt

Freshly ground black pepper

2 kumquats*

White balsamic vinegar

7 or 8 whole bonito flakes**

---

* Kumquats are tree fruit that look like miniature oranges, but unlike most citrus fruit, they have a sweet skin, which means you can eat them whole. They're around from late fall to early spring.

CELERY ROOT

celery juice, mascarpone, poppy seed

1 medium celery root

Some good olive oil

Kosher salt

Freshly ground black pepper

Half a lemon

White balsamic vinegar

1 celery stalk, plus a few inner celery leaves for garnish

40 grams (about 3 tablespoons) mascarpone

5 grams (1½ teaspoons) poppy seeds

Celery root is an unsung ingredient. This dish makes the most of its clean flavor and crunch, which is refreshing in a season dominated by roasted root vegetables. The juiced celery stalk isn't a superfluous add-on, either. It elevates the celery flavor of the whole dish. Consider it a really cheap, really good garnish.

Preheat the oven to 400°F. Use a sharp knife to cut off the tough outer layer of the celery root, being careful to remove as little of the flesh as possible. Cut about a quarter of the celery root off and set it aside. Using a mandoline or a very sharp knife, slice the rest of the celery root into pieces that are a maximum of ¼ inch thick. Cut the slices into slightly smaller irregular shapes. Toss them with a little olive oil and salt and pepper, and roast them on a sheet pan until they're just beginning to caramelize, about 30 minutes.

In the meantime, cut the remaining piece of raw celery root into small chunks and toss it with a big squeeze of lemon juice, a little olive oil, a splash of white balsamic vinegar, and salt and pepper. Juice the celery stalk in a juicer.

Take small spoonfuls of the mascarpone and spread them onto two plates, using two or three spoonfuls per plate. Arrange the roasted celery root on each plate and follow with the raw celery root. Spoon the celery juice onto each plate, and garnish with poppy seeds and a couple of celery leaves. Serve.

PASTA

Almost all of the recipes in this chapter call for fresh pasta. Which, reflexively, you probably understand. Fresh is always better. Homemade is always better. You shouldn't buy anything you can make. But clear your head of those thoughts for a minute. No one's asking you to make fresh pasta just to get into the spirit of making your own everything. There is a point to fresh pasta. The pasta in these dishes isn't just a vehicle for sauce, it's an ingredient in the dish. And as an ingredient you want it to be as good as all the other ingredients. You want it to be fresh and supple and flavorful.

The way we make pasta at the restaurant is pretty straightforward. The only thing we do that you probably can't do at home is vacuum-seal the kneaded ball of dough before letting it rest. The reason we do that is that it makes the dough easier to work with. That's crucial when you're making pasta for two hundred covers a night. It's not crucial at home.

The real trick and the God's honest truth is, the only way to make good fresh pasta is to make it over and over and over again. If you make it a few times a year, you're never going to be satisfied with the results. And the process will continue to seem labor-intensive enough that you'll probably continue making it only a few times a year. If you go on a blitz, a real pasta-making spree, cranking it out at least once a week for a couple of months, you will emerge good and fast at making fresh pasta. And from then on out, you *will* make it once a week because it'll be a piece of cake. Or a piece of really delicate maltagliati.

PASTA DOUGH

**MAKES 450 GRAMS
(1 POUND); SERVES 3 OR 4***

300 grams (2 cups plus
3½ tablespoons)
Tipo 00 flour**

6 large egg yolks

60 grams (¼ cup) room-
temperature water

All-purpose flour, for
rolling the dough

* The number of servings here
is approximate because it
depends on how much pasta
you want to eat. This dough
makes four good-size bowls of
pasta. You could also divide
the same amount among three
people without anyone feeling
overstuffed.

** This is Italian flour that's
much more finely milled than
American flour. It makes lighter
pasta with a really nice texture.

This dough is for delicate pastas—pappardelle, tagliatelle, maltagliati, and anything intended to be stuffed. It's light and eggy, and especially good with eggs from chickens that have been out foraging, which the free-roaming kind does from March through October. The yolk is more brightly colored and flavorful then than it is in the dead of winter, and the resulting pasta dough is a deep shade of gold.

If you roll the dough into thin sheets—for this dough, no matter what kind of pasta you're making with it, that means the thinnest setting on a pasta machine, or about 1/16 inch thick—lightly flour it, and layer it on a sheet pan between sheets of parchment paper, it'll keep in the refrigerator for up to two days. You can also freeze it for up to a month.

Sift the flour (this is particularly key if the flour's been sitting around a while or if it's been humid). On a work surface or in a big metal bowl, mound your sifted flour and make a well in the center.

Put the egg yolks and a splash of the water in the well. With your hands, break up the egg yolks and begin incorporating the flour into them a little at a time (if you're using a bowl, put a kitchen towel under the bowl so it doesn't spin around while you mix). Take your time. Work the mixture with your fingers and gradually pull in more flour from underneath and around it, adding more water if the dough seems dry.

When the dough starts to come together into a mass, transfer it to a dry surface and begin kneading it. Push it, pull it, and push it back down again. Put the palms of your hands into it. Work the dough firmly until it's one cohesive, smooth mass, about 10 minutes. Wrap it in a damp kitchen towel and let it rest at room temperature for half an hour. If

you're not using it immediately, wrap it in plastic wrap, refrigerate it, and use it within 12 hours.

Attach your pasta machine to the edge of a clean, long work surface. Divide the dough into 2 baseball-size balls. Flatten them slightly with your hand and dust them lightly with flour. Set the pasta machine to the widest setting and feed one ball of dough into it four or five times in a row. Adjust the setting to the next widest and feed the dough through three or four times. If the pasta cracks along the side, fold the cracked edge over and feed the sheet through the machine again to smooth it out. Adjust the machine to the thinnest possible setting and feed the dough through. The resulting sheet of pasta should be about $\frac{1}{16}$ inch thick—just short of being translucent. Repeat with the remaining ball of dough. Cover the sheets with damp towels.

EGGLESS PASTA DOUGH

This dough—a mix of all-purpose flour, semolina, and water—is for sturdy, thirsty pasta like orecchiette, pici, and trucidi. The pasta isn't meant to be dense, it's just meant to have body and bite. Uncut, the dough will keep in the refrigerator for up to 12 hours.

MAKES 530 TO 585 GRAMS
(ABOUT 1¼ POUNDS);
SERVES 3 OR 4
(SEE NOTE, PAGE 126)

180 grams (1⅓ cups plus 1 tablespoon) all-purpose flour

180 grams (1 cup plus 2 teaspoons) semolina flour, plus more for kneading

170 to 225 grams (¾ to 1 cup) room-temperature water

Combine the flours and mound them on a lightly floured work surface or in a big metal bowl. Make a well in the center and add ¾ cup water to it. With your hands, begin incorporating the flour into the water (if you're using a bowl, put a kitchen towel under the bowl so it doesn't spin around while you mix). How much water you end up using will depend on the humidity in your kitchen. Don't try to gauge the moisture in the air—just watch the dough. If it looks dry, add more water. When the dough starts to come together into a cohesive mass that's sticky but not tacky, stop adding water.

Transfer the dough to a dry work surface and begin kneading it. Dust the surface with semolina only if the dough sticks. Push the dough down, pull it, and push it back down again, kneading firmly for 5 to 10 minutes. The mass should be cleaner looking but still elastic and a little sticky. Wrap the dough in a damp kitchen towel and let it rest for 10 minutes. If you're not using it immediately, wrap it tightly in plastic wrap, refrigerate it, and use it within 12 hours.

LINGUINE

sea urchin, chili

100 grams (3½ ounces) sea
urchin tongues
(see note, page 166)

Some good olive oil

340 grams (12 ounces)
dry linguine*

2 garlic cloves, peeled
and smashed

A big pinch of chili
flakes

Sea salt, preferably
Maldon

* Look for "bronze dye extruded" dried pasta. That means it's been made according to a centuries-old Italian method that leaves it with a slightly rough surface. That surface makes sauces cling to the pasta really well.

It's probably hard to imagine having leftover sea urchin lying around. But that is, in fact, how this dish came into being. Most of the tongues—your buttery, briny reward for cracking open a sea urchin— had been put to other uses and there was a pile of pillaged sea urchin bodies and all this runny stuff lying around. The runny stuff and some roe went into a blender with olive oil and got tossed with linguine. The result was a revelation that's now an official greatest hit.

Put the sea urchin tongues in a blender with a couple of splashes of olive oil, and blend it for a few seconds until it's a smooth puree with the consistency of melted ice cream. Put the mixture in the refrigerator.

Put a pot of heavily salted water on to boil, and put three or four shallow bowls for serving in a 200°F oven to warm.

When the water is boiling, add the pasta to it. At the same time, coat a large sauté pan with olive oil. Set the pan over medium heat and add the garlic. Let the garlic color, and when the pasta is just about al dente, remove the garlic from the sauté pan and discard it, and take the sea urchin mixture out of the refrigerator.

Transfer the pasta from the pot to the sauté pan with tongs, and lower the heat. Add a splash of pasta water to the pan and give the pan a shake. Add a generous pinch of chili flakes.

Remove the pan from the heat and add another splash of pasta water and the sea urchin mixture, tossing it gently with the pasta and putting the pan back on the heat for a couple of seconds and then removing it again. You don't want to cook the sea urchin at all—much the way you don't want to cook the eggs when you're making a carbonara. You want the sauce to have a creamy consistency; if it doesn't, add a little more pasta water. When the pasta is well coated with the sauce, transfer it to the warmed shallow bowls. Sprinkle a little sea salt over each bowl and serve.

INDEPENDENT BOOKSELLERS

★

MᶜNALLY JACKSON

★

TEL (212) 274-1160
52 PRINCE ST, NYC
MCNALLYJACKSON.COM

PAPPARDELLE
black truffle, egg yolk, nasturtium

SERVES 3 OR 4

5 or 6 large egg yolks

Pasta dough
(page 126)

All-purpose flour, for
cutting the pasta

Kosher salt

Freshly ground black
pepper

Some good olive oil

A handful of nasturtium
leaves* (optional)

40 grams (about
1½ ounces) black
truffle**

Sea salt, preferably
Maldon

This is the Platonic ideal of pasta. It's rich and satisfying but really simple. The hardest work is making a nice light dough and shelling out for a nugget of black truffle.

Separate the eggs and let the yolks come to room temperature (reserve the whites for another use). Put a big pot of generously salted water on to boil.

Lay the rolled sheets of pasta on a floured surface and use a pizza cutter or a very sharp knife to cut them into ribbons ¾ inch to 1 inch wide. If you're using the pasta right away, cover it with a damp kitchen towel until you're ready to drop it in the pot. If you're not using it right away, lightly dust it with flour, layer it between pieces of parchment paper on a sheet pan, cover tightly with plastic wrap, and refrigerate for up to 8 hours.

Put the egg yolks in a blender with a generous pinch of kosher salt and a few grindings of black pepper; blend for 30 seconds. Put three or four shallow bowls for serving in a 200°F oven to warm.

Put a splash of olive oil in a large sauté pan and place it over medium heat. Drop the pasta into the pot of boiling water and boil it for 2 minutes. Using tongs, transfer the pasta gently from the pot to the sauté pan, taking a little pasta water along with it. Toss the pappardelle in the olive oil and remove the pan from the heat. Wait about 30 seconds to let the pan cool slightly. With the pan still off the heat, add the blended yolks. Toss the pappardelle with them, putting the pan back on the heat for a few seconds and then taking it off for a few seconds; you don't want the yolks to cook, but you do want them to be warm.

Divide the pasta among the warmed shallow bowls and garnish each with a drizzle of olive oil and a few nasturtium leaves. (If you're not using nasturtium leaves, give each bowl a generous grinding of black pepper.) Shave the truffle on top, sprinkle with a little sea salt, and serve.

* Nasturtium is a plant in the watercress family that's very easy to grow and has edible flowers and leaves. We grow a lot of it. And we use it a lot as a garnish because it has a really spicy zing and it's prettier than a grind of black pepper.

** Depending on when you look, you'll see summer black truffles or winter black truffles. The winter variety is a little more powerful than the summer, so you might want to use a little less. In either case, they're expensive. You will probably spend somewhere between $40 and $60 for a small truffle. But you'll have some left over. Store it in a paper bag in the refrigerator if you're using it within a few days, otherwise in a sealed glass jar in the freezer.

MALTAGLIATI
sungold tomato, parmigiano

Pasta dough
(page 126)

All-purpose flour, for
cutting the pasta

Some good olive oil

2 pints Sungold tomatoes,
washed

Kosher salt

Freshly ground black
pepper

80 grams (3 ounces)
parmigiano, finely
grated

There are all kinds of ways to combine tomatoes and pasta. Not a lot of them involve lighting a grill. But getting a char on Sungolds—an intensely sweet, tangerine-colored kind of cherry tomato—gives this pasta a smoky sweetness that makes it. At the restaurant we have a Japanese grill with a finer grate than the average Weber, so there's less risk of losing tomatoes. At home, you might want to use a grill basket. Or a few extra tomatoes just in case.

Lay the rolled sheets of pasta on a lightly floured work surface and crisscross them diagonally with a pizza cutter or a very sharp knife. (*Maltagliati* means "badly cut" in Italian, so don't be too fussy—you want scrap-like, roughly triangular pieces of pasta, slightly bigger than bite-size.) If you're not using the pasta right away, dust it lightly with flour, layer it between sheets of parchment paper on a sheet pan, cover tightly with plastic wrap, and refrigerate it for up to 8 hours.

Put the cut pasta in a big bowl, and using your hands, gently toss it with a splash of olive oil.

Get a charcoal or gas grill going on medium-low heat. Toss half of the tomatoes with a little olive oil and salt, and put them on the grill; if the tomatoes are small enough to fall through the grate on your grill, you might have to use a grill basket. Let the tomatoes cook slowly; they're done when their skin is blackening here and there and they look like they're starting to melt. Use a big metal spatula to transfer them to a bowl, and set them aside.

Put a large pot of generously salted water on to boil, and put three or four shallow bowls for serving in a 200°F oven to warm.

Halve the remaining tomatoes and use the back of a big spoon to push them through a fine-mesh strainer into a bowl. Strain what's in the bowl one more time. You should have a dark-colored tomato broth—thicker than tomato water but with no pulp. Season it to taste with salt and pepper.

Divide the tomato broth among the warmed shallow bowls. Drop the pasta into the pot of boiling water and boil for 2 minutes. Using tongs, transfer the pasta from the pot to a big bowl and quickly toss it with a splash of olive oil and about half of the parmigiano. Transfer the pasta to the warmed bowls. Scatter the grilled Sungolds over the pasta, and give each bowl a drizzle of olive oil. Grate the remaining parmigiano on top, and serve.

TRUCIDI

razor clam, bottarga

There's nothing wrong with littlenecks. They're sweet and juicy and briny—everything you want a clam to be. But razor clams have a delicate, more complex flavor. The broth for this pasta concentrates that flavor and the trucidi does an excellent job soaking it up. If you're into clams and you've only ever had littlenecks and steamers, this is a nice way to branch out.

Cut a chunk of dough a little bigger than a golf ball off the mass. Do not flour your work surface. With open palms, roll the chunk out into a long rope ½ inch in diameter. Cut the rope into pieces about 1½ inches long. Repeat until you've used all of the dough. Place a piece of pasta vertically in front of you. Hold a small knife flat over the pasta with the blade facing away from you. Turn the knife 45 degrees clockwise so all you can see of the pasta is a small triangle peeking out. Press the knife down on the pasta, putting some pressure on the blade but not so much that you cut through the pasta. Then drag the knife downward and to the left, keeping enough pressure on the pasta so that it doesn't move with the knife. The pasta should look like a loosely curled ribbon (in fact, the motion is the same as what you'd do to curl a ribbon). It may take you several tries to get the knife pressure right so that the knife moves but the pasta doesn't. Repeat with the remaining pasta, transferring the pieces to two sheet pans lined with parchment paper and loosely dusted with semolina as you go. Either use immediately or cover the sheet pans tightly with plastic wrap and refrigerate for no more than a few hours.

Razor clams should close when tapped together. If they don't close, they are not alive. Discard any clams that don't close. Use a paring

Eggless pasta dough (page 129)

Semolina, for dusting

20 razor clams (680 to 907 grams, 1½ to 2 pounds)

Some good olive oil

6 garlic cloves, peeled and smashed

1 leek, light green and white parts only, halved lengthwise, rinsed well, and thinly sliced, or 1 small yellow onion, finely chopped

Chili flakes

340 grams (1½ cups) dry white wine

Kosher salt

Half a lemon

25 grams (¾ ounce) bottarga (see note, page 88)

2 or 3 scallions, thinly sliced

knife to cut the meat out of the clams, leaving the dark flesh attached to the shell and removing the firm, white body. Rinse the white clam bodies in cold water and set all but four of them aside. Reserve all of the shells. Finely chop the four clams.

Put a big splash of olive oil in a medium pot and place it over medium-low heat. Add half of the garlic and let it cook until it begins to color. Remove the garlic and add the leek or onion, the finely chopped raw clams, a generous pinch of chili flakes and last, the razor clam shells. Turn the heat up to medium and add the wine. Bring the broth to a boil and let it go for 10 seconds. Turn the heat down to low. Add a pinch of salt, cover the pan, and let the broth simmer for 45 minutes to an hour, until it has reduced to the consistency of a very light sauce. The flavors should come together and no one flavor—like the wine—should be dominant. Taste and adjust the seasoning if necessary. Strain the finished liquid through a fine-mesh strainer.

Put a large pot of lightly salted water on to boil (because of the clams, this is one instance when you shouldn't heavily salt the pasta water), and put three or four shallow bowls for serving in a 200°F oven to warm.

Put a splash of olive oil in a large, deep sauté pan and set it over medium heat. Add the remaining garlic and another generous pinch of chili flakes. Let the garlic color a little, and then remove it and add the clam broth.

Drop the pasta into the boiling water and cook it for 4 minutes, until al dente. In the meantime, dress the reserved raw clams in a drizzle of olive oil and a pinch of salt. Using tongs, transfer the pasta from the pot to the sauté pan and turn the heat down to low. Toss the pasta gently in the broth, and then add a big squeeze of lemon juice and the reserved raw clams. Taste and adjust the seasoning if necessary. Toss again and divide among the warmed shallow bowls. Shave a little bottarga over each dish. Scatter the scallions over the top and serve.

AGNOLOTTI
taleggio, black truffle

Pasta dough
(page 126)

57 grams (¼ cup) heavy
cream

2 grams (½ teaspoon)
agar powder*

175 grams (6 ounces)
Taleggio (see note,
page 49)

Semolina, for the sheet
pan

40 grams (about
3 tablespoons) butter

30 grams (1 ounce)
black truffle (see note,
page 133)

A handful of nasturtium
leaves (see note,
page 133)

Freshly ground black
pepper

There's nothing crazy happening here. In fact, if you describe this dish simply you could be talking about something from a kids' menu: pasta stuffed with cheese. But save this one for the grown-ups. Taleggio has a pungent smell but a mild flavor—creamy and buttery with a very slight tang. It makes stuffed pasta that, instead of making you want less of it after a few bites, makes you want more.

Lay the pasta sheets on a work surface and cover them with damp towels.

In a small saucepan, heat the heavy cream over medium-high heat almost to the boiling point. Whisk in the agar and leave on the heat for another minute, until just boiling. Remove the pan from the heat and let it cool slightly.

In a blender, combine the Taleggio with the cooled cream and blend until combined. Transfer the mixture to a pastry bag fitted with a ¼-inch round tip (or a quart-size zipper-lock bag with one bottom corner snipped off).

Place a pasta sheet horizontally in front of you on a dry work surface. Squeeze the Taleggio mixture in one long toothpaste-width line along the length of the sheet, about ½ inch from the top edge of the sheet. Fold the top edge of the pasta up over the filling and press firmly to seal. Using a pizza cutter or a sharp knife, separate the filled tube from the rest of the pasta sheet by cutting along the line where the folded-over edge meets the rest of the sheet. Holding the thumb and fore-finger of one hand about 1 inch apart, push down on the tube, pinching it flat between 1-inch lengths of filling until you reach the end. Use a pizza cutter or a sharp knife to cut the pasta at each pinch. (If you want to give the agnolotti traditional crimped edges, you can use a pastry wheel here.) Transfer the agnolotti to a sheet pan dusted with semolina. Repeat with the remaining pasta. If you're not using the agnolotti right away, cover the sheet pan tightly with plastic wrap and refrigerate for up to 8 hours.

Put a big pot of heavily salted water on to boil, and put three or four shallow bowls for serving in a 200°F oven to warm.

In a large sauté pan over medium heat, melt the butter. When the butter begins to foam, gently shake the pan to keep the butter moving. Keep a close eye on it so it doesn't burn. After a few minutes, it should begin to turn brown and fragrant. Scrape the bottom of the pan with a wooden spatula a couple of times to prevent the milk solids from sticking. When the butter is a deep brown, remove the pan from the heat. Using a hand-held fine grater, grate three-quarters of the truffle over the butter.

Add the agnolotti to the boiling water and cook for 3 minutes. Use a slotted spoon to transfer the agnolotti from the pot to the pan containing the butter. Add a splash of pasta water, check the seasoning, and adjust if necessary. Shake the pan to toss the pasta, and when it's well coated, divide it among the warmed shallow bowls and finely grate the remaining black truffle over each one. Garnish each bowl with a few nasturtium leaves and a grinding of black pepper, and serve.

* Agar is a vegetable protein that acts like gelatin. It's used in all kinds of cooking as a thickener and temperature stabilizer. Here it prevents the cream from breaking down when it's stuffed in the pasta and cooked. You can find agar in powder form at Asian markets, health food stores, and online.

CITRUS MALTAGLIATI

Pasta dough
(page 126)

All-purpose flour, for
cutting the pasta

Some good olive oil

900 grams (about 2 pounds)
tangerines (or any
not-too-tart citrus that's
in season)

80 grams (2¾ ounces)
Pecorino Fiore Sardo,
finely grated (see note,
page 99)

A pinch of chili flakes

If you're tired of pasta, make this one. A while back, a deep dive into sixteenth-century Italian culinary history turned up the surprising combination of citrus with pasta. Apparently the luxury-hungry Medicis felt that anything *New World* was where it was at, and that included hard-to-find citrus and exotic spices. They were also more relaxed about the line between sweet and savory back then. They were onto something.

Lay the rolled sheets of pasta on a lightly floured work surface and crisscross them diagonally with a pizza cutter or a very sharp knife. (*Maltagliati* means "badly cut" in Italian, so don't be too fussy—you want scrap-like, roughly triangular pieces of pasta, slightly bigger than bite-size.) If you're not using the pasta right away, dust it lightly with flour, layer it between sheets of parchment paper on a sheet pan, cover tightly with plastic wrap, and refrigerate it for up to 8 hours.

Put the cut pasta in a big bowl, and using your hands, gently toss it with a big splash of olive oil.

Grate the zest of 3 tangerines and set the zest aside. Juice all of the tangerines; you should end up with about 2 cups of liquid.

Put a large pot of generously salted water on to boil, and put three or four shallow bowls in a 200°F oven to warm.

In a large sauté pan over medium heat, simmer the tangerine juice gently until it reduces by about half. This should take about 10 minutes.

Drop the pasta into the boiling water and cook it for 30 seconds. Use a slotted spoon to transfer the pasta from the pot to the sauté pan, along with half a ladle of pasta water. Give the pan a shake to get the pasta well covered in the liquid. Grate three-quarters of the pecorino into

the pan and add the pinch of chili flakes. Take the pan off the heat and give it a couple of shakes. Put it back on the heat and repeat. You want the cheese to emulsify a little in the liquid. Add the tangerine zest, toss, and divide the pasta among the warmed shallow bowls. Garnish each bowl with a drizzle of olive oil and a little of the remaining pecorino, and serve.

LAMB CARBONARA

mint

SERVES 3 OR 4

Some good olive oil

A quarter of the cured lamb breast (recipe follows), cut into thick dice

Freshly ground black pepper

3 egg yolks, at room temperature

340 grams (12 ounces) dry spaghetti (see note, page 130)

125 grams (4½ ounces) Pecorino Romano, finely grated

10 to 15 mint leaves (whole if small, coarsely chopped if large)

Lamb isn't hard to cure, and it's worth doing just for this pasta. You'll end up with a carbonara with an extra layer of richness that makes it even more satisfying than classic carbonara—especially on a really cold night.

Put a big pot of heavily salted water on to boil. Put a little bit of olive oil in a large sauté pan and set it over low heat. Add the diced lamb and several grinds of black pepper. Render the lamb slowly, over 6 to 8 minutes—you want it to be soft and tender, not crispy.

In the meantime, beat the egg yolks with a fork.

Drop the pasta into the boiling water and cook it for 10 to 11 minutes, until al dente. While it's cooking, put three or four shallow bowls for serving in a 200°F oven to warm.

Use tongs to transfer the pasta from the pot to the pan containing the lamb, and turn the heat off. (You can reserve some pasta water in case the pasta seems dry to you later on, but it's almost never necessary here.) Toss the pasta until it's well coated with the lamb fat. Add three-quarters of the pecorino and all of the mint leaves, and toss. Add the egg yolks and continue to toss until the pasta is well coated. Divide the pasta among the warmed shallow bowls and garnish with more cheese. Serve.

cured lamb breast

You'll have more here than you need for the carbonara. Use it however you want—cooked in thick slabs in a pan just like bacon, for instance.

In a big bowl, mix together the salt, brown sugar, garlic, thyme sprigs, and 5 or 6 coarse grinds of black pepper. Spread the mixture on a sheet pan and dredge the lamb breast in it, turning it and rubbing the mixture in to make sure it's well covered. Shake the excess mixture off the lamb and transfer the lamb to a clean sheet pan. Cover the pan tightly with plastic wrap and refrigerate it for 3 days, flipping it once a day. The meat should be firm to the touch.

Rinse the rub completely off the lamb and soak it for an hour in cold water. Pat it dry, place it on a sheet pan and wrap it loosely in plastic wrap. Refrigerate it for up to 24 hours to dry it completely. The cured lamb will keep in the refrigerator for up to two weeks.

* You don't see a lot of recipes that call for lamb breast. Probably because it's a long strip with a lot of fat and only a little meat on it; it's the part of the lamb where the ribs were attached. Ask for it—deboned—at the meat counter of a good supermarket or at a butcher.

**MAKES ABOUT 680 GRAMS
(1½ POUNDS)**

144 grams (1 cup) kosher salt

67 grams (½ cup) dark brown sugar, packed

6 garlic cloves, peeled and smashed

4 sprigs thyme, each torn in half

Freshly ground black pepper

1 boned lamb breast (about 680 grams/ 1½ pounds)*

GARGANELLI
squab

The everyday poultry we eat in America wouldn't lend itself to this kind of treatment. Squab, or young pigeon, is one of the tenderest birds you can eat. The flavor is rich and earthy but not aggressively gamy. At the restaurant, we hang, or dry-age, squab for about two weeks to concentrate that flavor and bring out a little funkiness. At home, your squab will still be intensely flavorful, so long as you cook it rare to medium-rare. We've given an alternative to sous vide for cooking the squab, but sous vide works especially well because it lets you cook the bird evenly all over. Either way, you'll end up with pasta that has amazing braised flavor, when in fact you didn't braise anything at all.

If you are making your own garganelli, you need a garganelli board or comb, which you can get online, and a dowel about the diameter of a pencil. It's a fun pasta to make once you get the hang of it. Lay the rolled sheets of pasta on a lightly floured work surface and use a pizza cutter or a very sharp knife to cut the pasta into 2-inch squares. Position a square like a diamond on the garganelli board. Lay the dowel horizontally on the bottom point of the diamond, press down lightly, and roll it upwards, curling the pasta around the dowel. Press down just before you finish to seal the upper corner to the rolled piece. Slide the piece off and repeat with the remaining squares. If you're using the pasta right away, cover it with a damp kitchen towel until you're ready to drop it in the pot. If you're not using it right away, lightly dust it with flour and layer it between pieces of parchment paper on a sheet pan, cover tightly with plastic wrap, and refrigerate for up to 8 hours.

continues

SERVES 3 OR 4

Pasta dough (page 126), or 350 grams (12 ounces) fresh or frozen garganelli

All-purpose flour, for shaping the pasta

1 (454- to 510-gram/ 16- to 18-ounce) cleaned squab*

Kosher salt

15 grams (1 tablespoon) duck fat for sous vide, or 1 (200-gram/ 7-ounce) container duck fat for cooking in the oven**

Some good olive oil

Unsalted butter

30 grams (2 tablespoons) canned tomato puree

Freshly ground black pepper

* There are squab being humanely raised on farms from California to Pennsylvania. Your butcher should be able to order a whole one, or you can buy one from an online supplier. We get our squabs whole and eviscerate them and remove the feet and head ourselves. Depending on the source, your bird is likely to come already dressed, which means that will have been done for you.

** If you're not cooking the squab sous vide, you will need the larger amount of duck fat called for in the ingredients. Buy at least a 7-ounce container's worth.

Breaking down a squab is simple. If your squab is already dressed, remove the pouch containing the organs from the squab. Rinse and dry the heart and liver. Finely chop them, and set them aside. Put the squab breast side up on a work surface, and cut along each breast to separate them from the keel (the top line of the backbone). Remove the legs and set them aside.

If cooking sous vide, salt the breasts lightly. Put them in a vacuum-seal pouch with a teaspoon of the duck fat. Vacuum-seal the bag and cook at 57°C/135°F for 20 minutes. Let them rest in the pouch for 10 minutes, then remove them, pat them dry, finely dice them, and set the meat aside. Lightly salt the legs and put them in a vacuum-seal pouch with the remaining duck fat. Vacuum-seal the bag and cook at 68°C/154°F for 25 minutes. Let them rest in the pouch for 10 minutes, then remove them, dry them off, and pull the meat off the bones.

To cook the squab in the oven, preheat the oven to 200°F. Lightly salt the breasts and legs and cover them all over with a thick layer of duck fat. Place the breasts and legs in a glass baking dish and put them in the oven. Remove the breasts after 15 minutes, finely dice them, and set aside. Let the legs cook another 1 hour and 45 minutes. When you can easily pull the meat off the bone with a fork, the legs are done. Remove them from the oven, dry them off, and pull off the meat.

Note: Squab meat is a nice rosy red color. If you don't use the meat right away, it will start to oxidize and turn brown. That's okay but it doesn't look as good. At the restaurant, we vacuum-seal the cooked meat to prevent that from happening. At home, you should just try to use the meat as soon as possible.

Put a big pot of heavily salted water on to boil, and put three or four shallow bowls in a 200°F oven to warm. If you did not sous vide the squab breast, lightly coat a large sauté pan with olive oil and place it over medium-high heat. When it's hot, add the diced breast and cook, tossing the pan, for 3 to 4 minutes until it firms up slightly but hasn't begun to color at all. Set the meat aside.

Place a large sauté pan over low heat, and as it warms, lightly coat it with butter. Add the tomato puree. Cook the garganelli in the boiling water for 30 seconds (if you're using frozen instead of homemade, cook it according to the package instructions). Use a slotted spoon to transfer it to the pan containing the tomato puree, and add a big splash of pasta water. Add the squab leg meat and toss. Turn up the heat just slightly to warm things through, but not high enough to color the meat.

Add the reserved breast meat and toss it with the pasta, and then add the liver and heart. If it seems dry, add another splash of pasta water. Check the seasoning and adjust it if necessary. Divide the pasta among the warmed shallow bowls and give each bowl a drizzle of olive oil and a few grinds of black pepper. Serve.

PICI
pig tail ragu

There are easier things to get than pig tails. But you should be able to get your hands on some through a good butcher shop or Asian market. Why would you do that? Because if you like pork, the tail is where you'll find some of the porkiest flavor. And cooked low and slow on the stovetop, pig tails make for a pretty mind-blowing ragu.

Cut a chunk of dough a little bigger than a golf ball off the mass. Do not flour your work surface. With open palms, roll the chunk out into a long rope about ¼ inch in diameter. Take the rope between two hands and roll it gently back and forth until it's lightly spiraled. Repeat with the remaining pasta, transferring the strands to a sheet pan lightly dusted with semolina as you go. Either use immediately or cover the sheet pan tightly with plastic wrap and refrigerate it for no more than a few hours.

Rinse and dry the pig tails and shave off any stray hairs with a sharp knife. Spread them out on a couple of baking sheets and salt them well.

Coat the bottom of a heavy-bottomed stockpot or a Dutch oven with olive oil and set it over medium heat. Brown the pig tails in batches—don't put so many in at a time that some of them aren't touching the oil—turning them with tongs to brown both sides and setting each batch aside when it's done.

When the pig tails are all browned, add the onion to the pot. Push it around with a wooden spoon and let it soften for a few minutes. Return the pig tails to the pot and add the wine and the tomatoes (the whole can—juice and all). Turn the heat down to low, cover the pot, and let it cook for 4 hours, giving it an occasional stir to keep it from getting too sticky at the bottom.

Eggless pasta dough (page 129)

Semolina, for dusting

900 grams (2 pounds) pig tails*

Kosher salt

Some good olive oil

1 medium onion, coarsely chopped

Half a bottle of dry red wine

1 (794-gram/28-ounce) can whole San Marzano tomatoes

A pinch of chili flakes

A chunk of Piave Vecchio** or parmigiano

A handful of parsley leaves, chopped

continues

* The pig tails you see at the market or get on order from a butcher should be dry and smooth, not sticky. Don't buy them otherwise.

** Piave Vecchio is an aged cheese from northern Italy that's like parmigiano but nuttier and a little more complex.

When you can see the meat starting to separate from the bones, turn the heat off and dump the meat onto rimmed sheet pans. Now that the bones are separated from the meat, you can remove them. Put on rubber gloves and pick through the meat to remove the bones, which are the size of TicTacs. Be careful not to toss out any skin or meat. When the meat is clean, put it back in the pot to warm on low heat.

Put a big pot of heavily salted water on to boil, and put three or four shallow bowls for serving in a 200°F oven to warm.

Coat a large sauté pan with olive oil, throw in a big pinch of chili flakes, and put it over medium-low heat. Add the pasta to the boiling water and cook until it's al dente, 3 to 4 minutes. Use a slotted spoon to transfer it from the pot to the sauté pan. Add the ragu and a splash of pasta water to the pan and toss the pasta a little. Check the seasoning and then divide the pici among the warmed shallow bowls. Garnish each bowl with a few shavings of cheese and the parsley. Serve.

ORECCHIETTE
oxtail ragu

Oxtails are easier to get than pig tails, and therefore you might have had an oxtail ragu before. This version isn't pulling any punches, but it does have something of a secret ingredient: dry-aged beef fat. The fat deepens and funkifies the flavor of the ragu in a way that makes it memorable and also kind of addictive. Here it's served with orecchiette but it works with any sturdy short pasta, with polenta, or just on its own, garnished with a few celery leaves.

Rinse the oxtail pieces, dry them well, and salt and pepper them really generously. Coat a heavy-bottomed stockpot or a Dutch oven with olive oil and put it over medium heat. Add the oxtail pieces—a batch at a time if you can't fit them all in the bottom of the pot—and brown them well on all sides, about 4 minutes per side, turning them with tongs as you go. Transfer the browned oxtails to a plate. Drain off all but 1 tablespoon of the fat in the pot, lower the heat, and add the aged beef fat to the pot. Let it render for 8 to 10 minutes.

Add the celery to the pot and turn the heat back up to medium. Let it cook for a few minutes. Then add the wine and push everything around in the pot with a wooden spoon, scraping up any brown bits left from the oxtail and mixing them in. Add the carrots, onion, and a big pinch of chili flakes to the pot, and let everything cook for a couple of minutes. Add the tomatoes (the whole can—juice and all) and the reserved oxtails. Turn the heat down to low, cover the pot, and let it cook for 4 to 5 hours, stirring occasionally to keep things from sticking to the bottom.

When the meat is falling off the bones, take the pot off the heat. Remove the oxtails from the pot. When it is cool enough to handle,

12 (3-inch) pieces oxtail

Kosher salt

Freshly ground black pepper

Some good olive oil

30 grams (2 tablespoons) dry-aged beef fat*

3 celery ribs, roughly chopped

Half a bottle of dry red wine

2 large carrots, roughly chopped

1 large onion, roughly chopped

Chili flakes

1 (794-gram/28-ounce) can whole San Marzano tomatoes

Eggless pasta dough (page 129)

All-purpose flour, for forming the dough

continues

pull the meat off the bones; set the meat aside. (Discard the fat, sinewy pieces, and the bones. Or give the bones to a dog.) Skim off the fat on the surface of the sauce, and return the meat to it. Season to taste with salt and pepper.

When you're ready to shape the pasta, put your mass of dough on an unfloured work surface. Break a golf-ball-size piece of dough off the mass and roll it out into a rope about ¾ inch in diameter and 12 to 14 inches long. Cut the rope into ¼-inch pieces. Dust your thumb with flour and press down on each piece of dough, twisting your thumb clockwise slightly. You should have an indented, imperfect round that looks a little like an ear. Repeat with the remaining dough and transfer the orecchiette to a semolina-dusted sheet pan.

Put a large pot of heavily salted water on to boil, and put three or four shallow bowls for serving in a 200°F oven to warm.

Coat a large sauté pan with olive oil, add a big pinch of chili flakes, and set it over medium-low heat. Add the pasta to the boiling water and cook until it's al dente, 5 or 6 minutes. Use a slotted spoon to transfer the pasta from the pot to the sauté pan, and add a big splash of pasta water. Check the seasoning, and divide the orecchiette among the warmed shallow bowls. Spoon the ragu over the pasta, garnish each bowl with a few shavings of cheese and a little parsley, and serve.

Semolina, for the sheet pan

A chunk of Piave Vecchio (see note, page 152) or parmigiano

A handful of parsley leaves, chopped

* We age our own beef at the restaurant, so we have dry-aged beef fat on hand. For you, the most direct way to get your hands on dry-aged beef fat is to buy a dry-aged steak and trim a little of the fat from it. That might seem extravagant, but cooked right (see page 245), the dry-aged steak will be worth it, and the reserved fat will be a very big bonus.

There is a period where you try to do things the way you've always done them. Not because you're stupid or in denial, but because you genuinely think that if everything had been working in such a magical, organic way, why couldn't it go on doing that? Why couldn't you scale up based on that model? A nice server is a nice server. Good pizza is good pizza. Positive energy makes up for a few organizational shortcomings. And as stoked as you are to be successful, as rad as it feels to have everyone come to your party every night, to have lines forming outside the thing that you built, you also feel a little bit like, fuck this. A little bit like: You guys are welcome to come here. We'll feed you and we'll host you and we'll show you a good time the way we do it. If you don't like it, well, don't come back.

And then some time passed. We grew up a little bit and realized that what we had was a restaurant, not some underground dinner party. We had some people who really wanted to be in buttoned-up hands.

They wanted their wait for a table to be concernedly reported and their server to have an appropriate level of seriousness about them. They wanted their water glasses filled the moment they were emptied. They wanted their wine to be uncorked and poured in the manner to which they were accustomed. We're not sure why they expected all of that, having made the journey they made to get to us, having walked down the block outside the restaurant, and having seen the place when they walked through the door. We're not even sure why they wanted it. But they did.

PROPOSAL FOR ROBERTA'S PIZZA UNDER THE BRIDGE

PAPPARDELLE
duck ragu

As good as meaty ragus can be, duck ragu is kind of king. You should have it once in a while. This one doesn't deviate from most classic duck ragus except for the fact that we lightly cure the legs to amplify the flavor, and at the very end, we spike it with a few shavings of very dark chocolate.

In a big bowl, mix the garlic cloves and thyme sprigs with the salt and 5 or 6 coarse grinds of black pepper. In a shallow glass container or on a sheet pan, spread half of the mixture in a thin layer. Put the duck legs on the salt mixture, and cover them with the remaining mixture. Seal the container or cover the pan tightly with plastic wrap and refrigerate it overnight—at least 8 hours and up to 12.

Lay the rolled sheets of pasta on a floured surface and use a pizza cutter or a very sharp knife to cut them into ribbons 1 to 1½ inches wide. If you're using the pasta right away, cover it with a damp kitchen towel until you're ready to drop it in the pot. If you're not using it right away, lightly dust it with flour, layer it between pieces of parchment paper on a sheet pan, cover tightly with plastic wrap, and refrigerate for up to 8 hours.

Remove the duck legs from the salt, rinse them, pat them dry, and let them come to room temperature.

Coat a big heavy-bottomed pot or a Dutch oven with olive oil and set it over medium-high heat. In batches, brown the duck legs well on each side, 3 to 5 minutes per side, and then remove them from the pot and set them aside. Pour off all but 2 tablespoons of fat. Lower the heat just a little and add the onion, celery, and carrots to the pot. Let them

4 garlic cloves, peeled

4 sprigs thyme

68 grams (½ cup) kosher salt, plus more as needed

Freshly ground black pepper

4 (400-gram/14-ounce) duck legs

Pasta dough (page 126)

All-purpose flour, for rolling the pasta

Some good olive oil

1 medium onion, finely chopped

3 celery ribs, finely chopped

2 medium carrots, finely chopped

340 grams (1½ cups) dry white wine

continues

1 (794-gram/28-ounce) can whole San Marzano tomatoes

35 grams (1¼ ounces) 80 to 90 percent dark chocolate, finely grated

A pinch of chili flakes

A chunk of Piave Vecchio (see note, page 152) or parmigiano

A handful of parsley leaves, chopped

soften for a few minutes, and then add the wine and give everything a stir. Add the tomatoes—juice and all—and stir. Break the tomatoes up a little with a wooden spoon. Return the duck legs, with their juices, to the pot, cover, and let everything simmer for 2 hours or more. The duck is done when the meat easily comes off the bone when it's prodded with a fork.

Turn off the heat, remove the duck legs from the pot, and let them sit until they're cool enough to handle. Then shred the meat, keeping about half the skin and fat and discarding the rest along with the bones. Return the meat, fat, and skin (try the skin first; some people don't like the texture. If you don't, don't add it) to the pot and set it over medium-low heat. Add the dark chocolate to the pot and stir. Check the seasoning and adjust if necessary.

Put a large pot of heavily salted water on to boil, and put three or four shallow bowls for serving in a 200°F oven to warm.

Coat a large sauté pan with olive oil, add a big pinch of chili flakes, and set it over medium-low heat. Put the pappardelle in the boiling water and cook for 2 minutes. Use tongs to transfer it from the pot to the sauté pan, and add a big splash of pasta water. Toss the pasta around a little and check the seasoning. Divide the pasta among the warmed shallow bowls and spoon ragu over each portion (there will be leftover ragu). Garnish with a few shavings of the cheese and a little parsley, and serve.

SEAFOOD

It's impossible to eat fish anymore without thinking about it. Which is a good thing if it means that everybody chooses to buy fish that was caught responsibly and, whenever possible, locally. And that everybody chooses not to buy endangered fish or fish that was caught in a way that damages an already damaged marine ecosystem. But the downside (relatively speaking) is that all the bad news on the marine front can make the process of buying fish paralyzing. There are plenty of accessible authorities on what fish you should buy and why.

Our best advice is to seek out the highest quality fish market near you and ask a few questions. Ask where a fish is from. Hope the answer is nearby, and if not, hope it's the U.S. Ask how it was caught—by dredge net, say, or hook and line. In most cases, hope the latter. If you don't like the answers, ask for an alternative. And lastly and maybe most importantly, get familiar with a few seasons for a few kinds of fish— mid-Atlantic black bass in the spring, bay scallops in the winter, squid almost anytime. If you see a fish that you know is in season, that's a good start.

Whenever possible, buy a whole fish. You'll know exactly what you're getting—it's not always easy to identify a fish once it's been filleted—and you'll be better able to inspect it for quality and freshness. Once you've identified a fish you feel good about buying, take a very close look at it. If you're buying a whole fish, its eyes should be crystal clear, not milky; its flesh should be firm (if the seller will let you poke it, the dent from your finger should disappear immediately); its gills should be bright red;

and it should smell like the ocean in the best possible way. If you're buying fillets, they should be firm; bright, not dull, if there's color to the flesh; and clean smelling.

Perfectly fresh fish is easy to cook. The best technique we know—and one repeated in many of the following recipes—is to leave the skin *and* the scales on the fillet (unless the scales are huge, which on very large fish they are), and sear it skin side down in a very hot pan coated with olive oil, keeping your hand on the fillet to keep it from buckling. When the skin is shatteringly crisp, put the pan in a 325°F oven and bake until the fish is just done, which will depend on the thickness of the fillet.

What follows are some ideas for what to do with perfectly cooked fish—oh, and sea urchin, shrimp, scallops, octopus, squid, cuttlefish, and crab. We are pretty into seafood.

SEA URCHIN

stracciatella, caviar, nasturtium granita

SERVES 4

---

100 grams (3½ ounces) stracciatella*

Some good olive oil

8 sea urchin tongues** (90 to 120 grams/3 to 4¼ ounces total)

Sea salt, preferably Maldon

Half a lemon

75 grams (⅓ cup) nasturtium granita (recipe follows)

15 grams (½ ounce) caviar, preferably American hackleback (otherwise whatever you like and can afford)

Sea urchin tops all of our lists. Favorites lists. Desert island lists. Last meal lists. If you haven't had it before, try it. Exotic as it looks and sounds (if you haven't had it), it's actually a familiar and beloved part of the food culture in lots of places—from the West Coast to the Mediterranean to Japan. For this recipe, we like San Diego sea urchin. It's sweeter and less aggressively briny than the East Coast variety. It's not local for us, but you know, neither is pecorino. It's a treat. And while we wholeheartedly endorse eating something this good just as it is, if you want to do it up, this is the way to do it.

Place a spoonful of stracciatella in each of four shallow bowls. Drizzle a little olive oil over each bowl. Place 2 sea urchin tongues on top of each portion of stracciatella, and sprinkle them with a few flakes of sea salt and a little lemon juice. Place a spoonful of granita and a smaller spoonful of caviar alongside the sea urchin in each bowl, and serve.

* Stracciatella is basically strands of mozzarella mixed together with cream. If you've had burrata, another cheese from the Puglia region of Italy, then you've had stracciatella—it's the creamy, mildly tangy center of burrata. If you can't find it, buy burrata instead.

** Sea urchin—or *uni*, as it's called in Japan—is popular enough now that you shouldn't have too much trouble finding it at big fish markets or online. You're going to get what are called "tongues"—so called because they look like tongues. The tongues are often referred to as roe, but they're actually gonads. For this recipe, you want 2 tongues per person.

nasturtium granita

You'll have more nasturtium granita than you need for this recipe. It has a clean, herbaceous flavor that goes amazingly well with vanilla ice cream for a not-too-sweet dessert. A few gelato cookies (see page 266) wouldn't hurt either.

Combine the water and sugar in a small saucepan over high heat, and stir to dissolve the sugar. When the liquid begins to boil, remove the pan from the heat and set aside.

Fill a big bowl about halfway with ice. Place another bowl on top of the ice. In a blender, blend the nasturtium leaves, cold water, and citric acid for about 30 seconds, until liquefied. Strain the liquid immediately into the chilled bowl (this helps keep the liquid from turning brown). Stir in about half of the simple syrup and a big squeeze of lemon juice. Taste and adjust with lemon juice and simple syrup as needed. The flavor should be clean and bright—not too sweet, too acidic, or too vegetal.

Pour the liquid into a loaf pan and put it in the freezer. Over the course of 2½ to 3 hours, stir the mixture with a whisk every 30 to 45 minutes. As it begins to go from slushy to icy, use a fork to stir and scrape it. When the mixture is about the texture of a snow cone, the granita is done. It will keep, covered, in the freezer for a week.

MAKES 480 GRAMS (2 CUPS)

225 grams (1 cup) water

115 grams (½ cup plus 1 tablespoon) sugar

27 grams (1 tightly packed cup) nasturtium leaves

200 grams (¾ cup plus 2 tablespoons) ice-cold water

A pinch of citric acid (to prevent the green nasturtiums from turning brown)

Half a lemon

SQUID

peach, scallion

SERVES 4

---

500 grams (a little over
    1 pound) cleaned baby
    or small squid

    Kosher salt

    Some good olive oil

  1 bunch scallions,
    washed, trimmed, and
    halved lengthwise

    Freshly ground black
    pepper

120 grams (½ cup) peach
    puree (recipe follows)

    Sea salt, preferably
    Maldon

You can use any squid here, but the smaller the squid, the tenderer it is and the easier to cook. If you can find baby squid, use those. As for the peaches, they're not just for fun. Imagine a forkful of hot salty squid mixed with delicate summer sweetness. Sounds good, right? Now go make it happen.

Separate the squid heads from the bodies and rinse both in cold water. Cut the bodies into slightly bigger than bite-size triangles, and score them lightly in a crosshatch pattern. Leave the tentacles whole. Dry the squid thoroughly with paper towels and salt them.

Coat a large sauté pan with olive oil and put it over almost high heat. Working in at least two batches to avoid overcrowding (in which case the squid will steam instead of sear), put the squid in the pan and toss them around, shaking the pan, until they are just barely starting to color, about 30 seconds. Transfer the squid to a paper-towel-lined plate.

Wipe out the sauté pan, coat it again with olive oil, and place it over almost high heat. Throw in the scallions and season them with salt and pepper. Sear them for about 30 seconds on each side, until they're just starting to color.

Put a big spoonful of peach puree in each of four shallow bowls. Put a serving of squid on top of each spoonful of puree. Garnish with a couple of scallion halves. Give each bowl a drizzle of olive oil and a tiny sprinkle of sea salt, and serve.

peach puree

You shouldn't have trouble finding a use for the extra puree here. We suggest having it with seared scallops, on crostini with ricotta, or, of course, with ice cream.

Peel the peaches and quarter them, discarding their pits. Put them in a blender with the olive oil, sugar, and a big pinch of salt. Blend for 1 minute or so, until you have a thick puree. It should be spoonable; if it's too thick, add a little more olive oil. Taste and adjust the seasoning— if the puree is too sweet, add a little more salt, or a little more sugar if otherwise. But you want it to taste like peaches, not sweetened peaches. The puree will keep in a sealed container in the refrigerator for a week.

**MAKES ABOUT 300 GRAMS
(ABOUT 1½ CUPS)**

3 ripe peaches

20 grams (2½ tablespoons) good olive oil

5 grams (1 teaspoon) sugar

Kosher salt

BAY SCALLOPS
meyer lemon, trout skin, poppy seed

We're not in the habit of calling out the provenance of our ingredients, but we never, ever use anything other than bay scallops from Nantucket, which are in season from late November until about late January. They're the sweetest, tenderest little bay scallops you can get. Honestly, they're like candy. And yes, of course they're delicious raw or barely sautéed in butter, but this is a fun way to dress them up.

Lay the skin on paper towels and let it dry at room temperature for an hour or two.

Preheat the oven to 100°F or to the lowest temperature possible. Put the skin on a sheet pan and bake it for 18 to 24 hours. It's done when it feels crisp to the touch.

When you're ready to prepare the scallops, fill a heavy-bottomed pot with 4 inches of canola oil. Using an accurate thermometer, heat the oil to 350°F.

Fry the skin in the oil for a couple of seconds, and transfer it to a paper-towel-lined plate. When it's cool enough to handle, break it into bite-size pieces.

Let the scallops come to room temperature and lightly salt them. Coat a large sauté pan with olive oil and place it over almost high heat. Add the scallops and sauté them, shaking the pan now and then, for 1 minute depending on their size. They're done when they're just starting to look opaque instead of translucent and beginning to color. Give the pan 3 big squeezes of lemon juice and divide the scallops among four shallow bowls. Garnish them with the poppy seeds and a few pieces of crispy trout skin. Serve.

SERVES 4

Trout skin*

Canola oil

450 grams (about 1 pound) Nantucket bay scallops

Kosher salt

Some good olive oil

2 Meyer lemons

35 grams (2½ table-spoons) poppy seeds

---

* The way crispy trout skin came to be a part of this dish at the restaurant is that we were smoking our own trout for a salad and had a lot of trout skin lying around. We tried frying it and found that it made an amazingly flavorful, crispy garnish. The smoked trout you can buy in stores almost always comes with skin on it. You could also buy a small (454-gram/1-pound) whole trout and get your hands on the skin that way. In any case, you don't need a lot for this recipe: just one strip of skin that's a few inches wide.

DIVER SCALLOP
plum juice, lardo, sea beans

SERVES 4

---

16 u/10 or u/15 diver
  scallops*

  Kosher salt

6 ripe, red-skinned plums

  A small handful of
  sea beans**

1 lemon

  Some good olive oil

16 paper-thin slices of
  lardo***

Diver scallops are just that. Scallops that are hand-harvested by a scuba diver, which as scallop-harvesting methods go, is the least disruptive to marine ecosystems. If you can't find divers, look for dayboats. "Dayboat" means that the boats that harvested the scallops returned to the shore at the end of the day instead of staying out on the water for days or weeks; in other words, the scallops are fresh. When they're as fresh as they can possibly be, scallops are unbeatable. The sweet-tart of the plum here complements their sweetness and while it might seem like overkill, the lardo delivers a little saltiness and a lot of richness that brings everything together.

Prepare a bowl of cold salted water. Remove and discard the muscles from the scallops—the little nub of flesh where the scallop was attached to its shell. Drop the trimmed scallops into the salted water and move them around a little to get rid of any sand. Rinse and pat them dry. Let the scallops come to room temperature, and then lightly salt them on both sides.

In the meantime, juice the plums. You can do this using a juicer or you can just cut them in a large dice, put the diced plum in a mesh strainer, and press on it with the back of a spoon to extract the juice. You should have enough for 2 tablespoons of juice per person: ½ cup in all. In a small bowl, toss the sea beans with a squeeze of lemon juice and a pinch of salt.

Coat a large sauté pan well with olive oil and place it over almost high heat. Put the scallops in the pan (do this in two batches to avoid crowding the pan) and don't touch them. After 1 to 1½ minutes, flip them and

cook them for 1 to 1½ minutes on the other side. They should begin to caramelize a little on both sides. Stick a metal probe into one of the scallops to check for doneness. If it comes out cold, cook them a little longer. If it comes out warm, they're done. (The cooking time will vary depending on the size of the scallops.) Transfer the scallops to a paper-towel-lined plate.

Put 4 small spoonfuls of plum juice in each of four shallow bowls. Place a scallop on top of each spoonful of juice, and drape a piece of lardo over it; the lardo will start to melt a little. Garnish each bowl with some sea beans, and serve.

* The designations u/10 and u/15 refer to the scallops' size. The "u" stands for "under" and indicates that fewer than 10 (or 15) scallops will make 1 pound. If 10 or fewer of the scallops make a pound, those are good-size scallops.

** Sea beans aren't seaweed. They're a succulent that grows near salt marshes and beaches in warmer weather. They have a salty kick and a clean, grassy flavor. They're showing up more at high-end supermarkets, but if you can't find them, you can substitute baby arugula here.

*** Lardo is fat from the thick layer on a pig's back that's been cured in salt, herbs, and dried spices. You can get it at Italian markets, good butchers, and online.

SOFT-SHELL CRAB

spicy mayo, herbs

SERVES 4

---

8 jumbo soft-shell crabs

Canola oil

280 grams (1 cup) instant flour, such as Wondra, or 140 grams (1 cup) all-purpose flour

Kosher salt

Freshly ground black pepper

1 lemon

1 lime

A big handful of mint leaves

2 jalapeños, sliced into thin rings

110 grams (½ cup) spicy mayo (recipe follows)

A small handful of chives, cut into matchstick-length pieces

4 scallions (green parts only), sliced in ¼-inch-thick rings

Soft-shell crabs don't ask for a lot. Toss them in well-seasoned flour, deep-fry them until golden, and if you're us, keep them on the menu all day—and on weekends during brunch, as a sandwich (if you have some nice potato rolls handy, go for it)—for as long as you can. The only place we haven't put them yet is on a pizza.

Take your crabs out of the refrigerator and let them come to room temperature.

Fill a heavy-bottomed pot with 4 inches of canola oil and set it over high heat. Using an accurate thermometer to check the temperature, heat the oil to 350°F.

In a big bowl, mix the flour with 2 generous pinches of salt and several grindings of black pepper. In a small bowl, use your fingers to toss a few big squeezes each of lemon and lime juice with the mint and jalapeños.

If your crabs are damp, pat them dry with paper towels. Toss them, a couple at a time, in the flour mixture until they're well coated, separating the legs to make sure they get coated too. Put the crabs in the oil and fry them for about 30 seconds on each side, until golden. Transfer them to a paper-towel-lined sheet pan.

Place a generous spoonful of spicy mayo on each plate and follow with 2 crabs each. Give all the crabs a little sprinkle of salt and a squeeze of lemon. Garnish each plate really generously with the mint and jalapeño mixture, and with the chives and scallions. Serve.

spicy mayo

Preheat the broiler. Broil the chilies until they're blackened on all sides, turning them as you go, 10 to 12 minutes. Let them cool and then remove the skins, cores, and seeds.

In a blender or in a bowl using a hand blender, combine the egg yolks with the lemon juice and ground mustard until well combined.

Add a few drops of the oil to the egg mixture, and blend or whisk to combine. In as slow a dribble as possible, continue to add the rest of the oil, blending constantly. When the mayo starts to look thick and shiny, stop adding oil. If you've added all the oil and it seems too thick, thin it out with a splash of water. Add the salt and the roasted chilies and blend just until combined. The spicy mayo will keep in the refrigerator for up to five days.

MAKES 280 GRAMS
(ABOUT 1½ CUPS)

2 fresh chilies*

2 large egg yolks

9 grams (1 tablespoon) freshly squeezed lemon juice

A pinch of ground mustard

285 grams (1¼ cups) canola, safflower, or vegetable oil

A big pinch of kosher salt

* The kind of chilies you use should depend on how much heat you like. We like a habanero—that's pretty spicy. You can use serranos, bird's eyes, cherry bombs, or, if you don't like much heat, jalapeños.

OCTOPUS

black garlic, treviso

Some good olive oil

8 garlic cloves, peeled

2 (1.4- to 1.8-kilogram/ 3- to 4-pound) Spanish octopus, cleaned

8 sprigs thyme

8 black garlic cloves*

Kosher salt

Half a head of Treviso, Tardivo, or radicchio (see page 112), washed, leaves separated

Freshly ground black pepper

* Black garlic is just long-fermented garlic. It has a mellow flavor that's something like roasted garlic and a kind of deep, dark, vinegary tang.

Perfectly cooked octopus is so different from octopus that's cooked just okay—a little over, a little under—that it might as well be a completely different animal. Which is why we don't provide you with any alternative cooking method to sous vide here. It isn't a great way to cook a lot of things, but it's a really good way to cook octopus. If you're able, try it.

Fill a small saucepan about a third of the way up with olive oil and set it over medium-low heat. When the oil is warm, add the white garlic cloves. Leave them for 10 minutes (just long enough to take the raw edge off the garlic) and then turn off the heat and remove the cloves. Set the garlic cloves and the garlic oil aside separately.

Put a large pot of water on to boil. Use a sharp knife to cut the heads off the octopus, just below the eyes. Discard the heads. Prepare ice baths in two large bowls. When the water is boiling, add the octopus tentacles and blanch them for no more than 10 seconds. Plunge the octopus into the ice baths.

Place 2 tentacles in each of eight sous-vide bags. Add to each bag a spoonful of the garlic olive oil, a thyme sprig, and a blanched garlic clove. Vacuum-seal the bags and cook the octopus at 81°C/178°F for 5 hours.

In the meantime, puree the black garlic in a blender with about ⅓ cup olive oil. You should end up with a thick puree. Refrigerate the puree until you're ready to prepare the octopus.

When the octopus is done, remove it from the sous vide bags and dry it off. Sprinkle each tentacle with a very little bit of salt.

Coat a large sauté pan with olive oil and place it over almost high heat. Brown the tentacles in batches, 1 to 1½ minutes on each side, until they're lightly colored. Be careful not to overbrown them.

Coat another large sauté pan with olive oil and place it over almost high heat. Add the Treviso leaves and season them with a little salt and pepper. Barely wilt the leaves, about 30 seconds.

Put a big spoonful of the black garlic puree on each of four plates. Divide the octopus among the plates and garnish with the wilted Treviso leaves. Serve.

CUTTLEFISH
pomelo, chili, hyssop

Cuttlefish are relatives of squid, but they're a little sweeter and a little meatier. Their name refers to the cuttlebone, a bone in their head that helps them maintain buoyancy. The cuttlefish you can find in America are almost always from the Mediterranean. In other words, not from around here. We don't have them on the menu all the time, but we do as often as we can in good conscience—usually in deep winter, around the start of pomelo season. Cuttlefish are good with almost any citrus, but mildly sweet pomelo is their soul mate.

Separate the cuttlefish bodies from the tentacles. Use a sharp knife to remove the beaks, then rinse the heads and tentacles in cold water and pat them dry. Cut the heads into ribbons ¾ to 1 inch wide. Salt and pepper the ribbons and tentacles well. Set aside.

Use a sharp knife to peel the pomelo, completely removing the skin and white pith. Supreme 4 segments: run a small sharp knife along both sides of each segment and gently peel away the outer membrane. Slice all 4 segments crosswise into thirds. Set the rest aside for squeezing.

Set a large sauté pan over high heat. When the pan is smoking hot, add a big splash of olive oil and then the cuttlefish. Shake the pan to toss the cuttlefish and cook for 30 seconds to 1 minute, until the cuttlefish is barely starting to color and is no longer translucent. Transfer to a bowl.

Squeeze the pomelo into the bowl—you want four big squeezes of juice. Add the pinch of chili flakes and the supremed pomelo, and toss everything together with your hands. Divide the cuttlefish among four shallow bowls, and garnish with a drizzle of olive oil and a few hyssop leaves. Serve.

SERVES 4

350 grams (12 ounces) cuttlefish

Kosher salt

Freshly ground black pepper

1 pomelo or oro blanco (see note, page 187), or 4 mandarin or Cara Cara oranges

Some good olive oil

A pinch of chili flakes

A very small handful of hyssop leaves*

---

* Hyssop is an herb with a strong anisey flavor. We use it because it makes for a nice contrast here and because we happen to have it growing out back. If you don't and you can't get your hands on any, you can use fennel fronds or fresh oregano leaves as garnish instead.

SMOKED SABLEFISH

meyer lemon, cucumber, english muffin

3.4 kilograms (3½ quarts) water

575 grams (3⅔ cups) kosher salt, plus more as needed

175 grams (¾ cup) sugar

494 grams (1 pound) sablefish belly or loin,* skin on and bones removed

2 to 3 cups alder wood chips

Unsalted butter

4 English muffins (recipe follows)

3 Kirby cucumbers, peeled and diced

1 lemon

Some good olive oil

Meyer lemon aioli (recipe follows)

Max Sussman, a former chef de cuisine at Roberta's, came up with this sandwich. He loves to smoke things. Sometimes, if you're talking to him about something or other and he just kind of stares at you, you can be pretty sure he's wondering what you would taste like if he smoked you for eight hours to an internal temperature of 158°F. If you haven't smoked anything yourself before, try it. You might not go as crazy as Max for it, but you'll want to do it again.

Mix the water, salt, and sugar together in a stockpot and set it over high heat. Bring the liquid to a boil and then turn off the heat. Let the liquid cool completely. Refrigerate until well chilled.

Submerge the sablefish completely in the chilled brine and let stand at room temperature for 45 minutes. Remove from the brine, pat the fish dry, and refrigerate uncovered until completely dry (ideally overnight).

Soak the wood chips in water for at least 20 minutes. Drain.

If you have a charcoal grill, move the coals to one side of the grill and heat them until they ash over. Put the chips directly on the coals and put the fish, skin side down, on the side of the grill opposite the coals. Close the lid and open the vent over the fish.

If you have a gas grill and a smoker box, put the chips in the box and place it over direct medium heat. Heat the chips until they start to smoke, 5 to 10 minutes. If you don't have a smoker box, put the chips on a sheet of aluminum foil, wrap them loosely, and poke holes in the top of the foil. Place the package on direct heat until the chips begin to smoke. Smoke the sablefish using indirect heat (place it on the grate but not directly over the flame).

To make a stovetop smoker, line the inside of a large wok with heavy foil. Place the wood chips in the wok. Make a drip pan by placing a heavy piece of foil over both the chips and the bottom of the wok. (Make sure it doesn't extend up the sides.) Set a 10- to 11-inch round baking rack over the drip pan. Place the fish, skin side down, on the grate, cover the smoker, and set the heat to high. When smoke appears, lower the heat to medium-high.

Smoke the sablefish for 35 to 40 minutes, adding more alder wood chips as necessary to keep the smoke coming, until the flesh is firm to the touch and looks opaque.

Let the fish cool. Then remove and discard the skin, and cut it into five or six 3- to 4-ounce pieces. (If you're making sandwiches for four, you'll have a little fish left over; it will keep in the refrigerator for a week. Make more sandwiches or add it to salads and breakfast spreads.)

Preheat the oven to 350°F. Place the sablefish for the sandwiches on a sheet pan and put it in the oven just to warm it. Melt a little butter. Use a serrated knife to score each English muffin around the rim. Split the muffins the rest of the way with a fork.

Set a large sauté pan over medium-low heat. Brush the split sides of the muffins with the melted butter and cook them, buttered side down, in the sauté pan until they're golden brown.

In a small bowl, toss the cucumber with 2 big squeezes of lemon juice, a pinch of salt, and a splash of olive oil.

Spread a spoonful of aioli on the split sides of each English muffin. Place a few spoonfuls of cucumber on the bottom of four muffin halves. Top each with a piece of sablefish, add the muffin top, and serve.

* Sablefish, also called black cod, is a relatively abundant fish from the North Pacific with buttery white flesh that's perfect for smoking. Some seafood watch organizations advise buying wild-caught sablefish from Alaska or British Columbia over anywhere else because of fishing practices. If you can't find belly, which is slightly fattier, loin will do just fine.

english muffins

MAKES 10 MUFFINS

11.5 grams (1 tablespoon plus ⅜ teaspoon) active dry yeast

900 grams (6½ cups minus scant 1 tablespoon) all-purpose flour, plus more for dusting

300 grams (1⅓ cups) room-temperature water

380 grams (1½ cups plus 1 tablespoon) whole milk, warmed to 80°F

20 grams (1 tablespoon plus 2 teaspoons) sugar

25 grams (2 tablespoons) distilled white vinegar

12 grams (2½ teaspoons) canola or other neutral oil

15 grams (1 generous tablespoon) baking powder

12 grams (1½ table-spoons) kosher salt

Cornmeal, for dusting

Unsalted butter

In a bowl, mix 1.5 grams (⅓ teaspoon) of the yeast, 300 grams (2 cups plus 2 heaping tablespoons) of the flour, and the room-temperature water together until there are no dry bits; this is called the *poolish*, or starter dough. Place it in a container that will allow the mixture to expand three times in volume. Let rest, covered with a kitchen towel, at room temperature for at least 8 and up to 12 hours.

After this time, in a large mixing bowl, whisk together the remaining yeast with the milk, sugar, vinegar, and oil. Add the poolish to this mixture.

In a separate bowl, mix the remaining flour with the baking powder and salt. Using a wooden spoon, combine the dry and wet ingredients together. Cover with a kitchen towel and set aside in a warm spot to rise until more than doubled in volume, about 3 hours.

Turn the dough out onto a floured surface, and pat it down with floured hands until it's about 1 inch thick. Use a 3¾-inch round cutter to cut muffins out of the dough. Place the muffins on a sheet pan that has been lined with parchment paper and dusted with cornmeal. Let the muffins sit for 10 to 15 minutes.

Ideally, cook the muffins on an electric griddle set to 350°F. If you don't have one, set two large nonstick sauté pans or two cast-iron skillets over medium heat. Grease the cooking surface lightly with butter and dust it with cornmeal. Cook the muffins for 5 to 8 minutes per side, turning them when the first side is done—each side should be a deep golden brown. Stored in an airtight container at room temperature, the muffins will keep for a week.

meyer lemon aioli

You'll have a little more aioli than you need here. It's delicious with anything fried, but especially seafood and potatoes.

In a food processor or using a whisk, mix together the vinegar, mustard, egg yolk, garlic, water, and salt. Add a few drops of the olive oil and blend or whisk to combine. Very slowly add the rest of both oils, blending or whisking constantly, until the aioli is emulsified. Stir in the lemon zest, juice, and dill, and check the seasoning, adding more salt or lemon juice as needed. The aioli will keep in the refrigerator for up to five days.

MAKES 302 GRAMS
(1¾ CUPS)

15 grams (1 teaspoon) red wine vinegar

3 grams (¾ teaspoon) Dijon mustard

1 large egg yolk

1 small garlic clove, peeled and minced

10 grams (2¼ teaspoons) water

1.5 grams (½ teaspoon) kosher salt

90 grams (¼ cup plus 2 tablespoons) good olive oil

300 grams (1½ cups) canola oil

Grated zest of 1 Meyer lemon

Juice of half a Meyer lemon

30 grams (2 tablespoons) chopped dill

MAINE SHRIMP
oro blanco, chili, black pepper

There is a small window in which to get these guys. Seize it. Maine shrimp are sweet little pink shrimp that are in season from late December through mid-January—right when you're in need of a gift. (They're so small and tender that you can and should eat the whole thing— head and all.) If you can't get them at a fish market near you, you can have them shipped. Decadent (and un-eco) maybe, but worth it.

Grate the zest from half of the oro blanco and set it aside. Use a sharp knife to peel the oro blanco, and set a few segments aside for squeezing. Supreme the remaining segments: run a small sharp knife along both sides of each segment and gently peel away the outer membrane.

In a big bowl, toss the shrimp with salt and pepper to taste. Coat a large sauté pan generously with olive oil and set it over medium-high heat. Put the shrimp in the pan one at a time. (You may need to sauté them in batches or in two different pans to avoid overcrowding the pan.) The shrimp will release a lot of moisture and that's okay; you don't want them to caramelize. After 30 seconds, flip the shrimp and cook them for another 30 seconds. Remove the pan from the heat and add a few big squeezes of oro blanco juice, a big pinch of chili flakes, several grinds of black pepper, and a splash of olive oil. Dump the contents of the pan, pan juices included, into a big bowl. Add the oro blanco supremes, toss, and check the seasoning.

Divide the contents of the bowl among four shallow bowls, or just serve the shrimp in one big shallow bowl or on a platter. In either case, garnish with a squeeze of oro blanco juice and the reserved zest.

SERVES 4

---

1 oro blanco,* pomelo, or pink grapefruit

450 grams (about 1 pound) Maine shrimp

Kosher salt

Freshly ground black pepper

Some good olive oil

A pinch of chili flakes

* Oro blancos are a cross between pomelo and white grapefruit. They have a nice sweet-tart flavor and they share a short, sweet winter season with Maine shrimp.

BLACK SEA BASS

parsnip, celery root, bonito broth

SERVES 4

Some good olive oil

1 small celery root,
   peeled and quartered

2 large carrots, peeled,
   trimmed, and halved

1 onion, quartered

2 parsnips, peeled,
   trimmed, and halved

Lukewarm water

1 (4-inch) piece kombu*

9 grams (1 cup) bonito
   flakes (see note,
   page 121)

4 (170- to 227-gram/
   6- to 8-ounce) black sea
   bass fillets,** skin and
   scales on

Kosher salt

20 grams (¾ ounce)
   dulse***

* Kombu is edible kelp that's
used for noodle broths and
all kinds of other things in
Japan. You can find it at Asian
markets, in the Asian section of
good supermarkets, or online.

This dish is bare-bones simple but rich in flavor—and more comforting and nourishing than anything called "comfort food" we've ever come across.

Coat the bottom of a large heavy-bottomed pot with olive oil and set it over medium-high heat. Add three-quarters of the celery root, the carrots, onion, and parsnips, and cook until they're just beginning to brown, about 10 minutes. Fill the pot about three-quarters full with lukewarm water and return it to the stove. Bring the water to a boil, lower it to a simmer, and let it simmer for 45 minutes to an hour.

Strain the broth through a fine-mesh strainer and return it to the pot. Add the kombu and bring to a simmer over medium heat. Remove the kombu as soon as the broth simmers, and strain the broth again through a fine-mesh strainer.

Return the broth to the pot, set it over high heat, and bring it back up to a boil. Turn off the heat, add the bonito flakes, and let the broth sit for 30 minutes. Then strain it again through a double layer of cheesecloth. Set it aside until you're ready to prepare the fish, and then put the broth over medium-low heat to warm it and check the seasoning. It shouldn't need salt, but you can adjust to taste.

Preheat the oven to 300°F. Bring the fish to room temperature and lightly salt it all over. Coat a large nonstick sauté pan with olive oil and set it over medium heat. Sear the fillets one at a time: Put the first one in the pan, skin side down, and keep your hand on it to keep it from buckling. Slowly raise the heat to almost high. After about 2 minutes, the fish should no longer stick to the pan and the skin should be crisp. Transfer it to a rimmed sheet pan and repeat with the remaining fillets.

Put them in the oven and bake for about 4 minutes. Check for doneness by inserting a metal skewer into one of the fillets. If it's cold, let the fish cook another minute. If it's warm, the fish is done.

Pour a ladle (about 1 cup) of warmed broth into each of four shallow bowls. Put a black bass fillet in each bowl, garnish with a little shaved raw celery root and dulse, and serve.

***Dulse is a dark red seaweed from the northern Pacific and Atlantic. In addition to being incredibly rich in vitamins and minerals, it has a nice briny flavor.

** Black sea bass isn't the same thing as Chilean or anything else typically called sea bass on menus. "Sea bass" is a catchall term used for a lot of bigger fish, many of which are overfished or unsustainably caught. Black bass is a smaller fish from the U.S. mid-Atlantic. At your fish market, ask specifically for black sea bass, which is sometimes called Atlantic sea bass or black perch. If you can't get it, you can use striped bass, which has a less delicate flavor, or a nice piece of cod.

MACKEREL

cranberry-ginger granita

115 grams (½ cup) sake

115 grams (½ cup) water

8 (3-inch) pieces kombu (see note, page 188)

4 (170-gram/6-ounce) mackerel fillets, skin on

Kosher salt

Rice vinegar

1 lemon

120 grams (½ cup) cranberry-ginger granita (recipe follows)

Oily fish like mackerel is lovable for a couple of reasons. One, it has rich, meaty flavor that doesn't need much of anything but the punch of something bright and acidic. Two, it's refreshingly guilt-free. Almost all oily fish, like mackerel and sardines, are abundant and more than okay to eat.

In a bowl, combine the sake with the water. Put the kombu in the bowl and leave it for a few minutes, then remove it and pat it dry.

Season the mackerel fillets well with salt and wrap each of them in kombu, using 2 pieces per fillet. Refrigerate the wrapped fillets for at least 8 hours and up to 12.

Fill a shallow bowl three-quarters full with rice vinegar. Unwrap the fish and rinse it in the bowl of rice vinegar; this will prevent it from being too salty. Pat the fish dry with paper towels.

If you have a kitchen torch (these are easy to find and nice to have around—get one!), use it to lightly crisp the skin all over. (You've basically cured the fish by salting it and refrigerating it for 8 hours. The kombu infused it with flavor. It doesn't need to be cooked now, just brought to room temperature and torched to crisp the skin and warm the flesh a little.) If you don't have a kitchen torch, heat a charcoal grill until the coals gray over, lightly oil the skin, and sear the fish skin side down until the skin is crisp and dark. Alternatively, set a cast-iron pan over high heat and lightly oil the skin on the mackerel. Put the fillets in the pan, skin side down, for 20 to 30 seconds, until the skin is crisped.

Slice the fish on the bias into thin slices—about ½ inch thick. Divide the fish among four plates and give each serving a squeeze of lemon. Put a big spoonful of granita next to the fish on each plate, and serve.

cranberry-ginger granita

Put the cranberries and sugar in a medium heavy-bottomed pot with just enough water to cover them. Add the ginger. Bring the water to a boil, lower the heat, and simmer, uncovered, for 25 to 30 minutes. The cranberries will start to burst.

Turn off the heat and let everything cool for a few minutes. Then strain the mixture through a fine-mesh strainer into a loaf pan, pressing on the berries with the back of a spoon, and put it in the freezer. Over the course of 2½ to 3 hours, stir the mixture with a whisk every 30 to 45 minutes. As it begins to go from slushy to icy, use a fork to stir and scrape it. When the mixture is about the texture of a snow cone, the granita is done. It will keep, covered, in the freezer for a week.

MAKES 240 GRAMS (1 CUP)

342 grams (3 cups) fresh cranberries

115 grams (generous ½ cup) sugar

15 grams (½ ounce) fresh ginger, peeled and cut into matchsticks

A little while after that first Times review, we got gas. Up until then, if it wasn't pizza, Carlo was cooking it on two portable cassette burners and a toaster oven. He was in the weeds when there were three orders up. But he was managing, somehow, to make some nice food.

He was alone back there. For probably much longer than was healthy for anyone, Carlo's only company in the kitchen was a friend of ours, a musician named Sam Jayne, who washed dishes. It took him so goddamn long to wash dishes that almost every night, someone had to volunteer to babysit Sam in the kitchen for a couple of hours after we closed while he finished up. But during relatively more normal hours back there, Carlo experimented. He'd worked in the kitchen at some crappy restaurants on Long Island and he'd cooked under a legitimate chef-owner at a bar with pretty refined food in SoHo. That was it. So he took his butane burners and his toaster oven—there was a range but until we got gas, almost a year in, it was useless—and he messed around.

The menu expanded beyond the first cave drawing—Meat Plate, Cheese Plate, Combo Plate, Greens with Gorgonzola & Roasted Walnuts—according to how the equipment and capacity of the back kitchen expanded. That first winter, he did oxtail ragu because he could make it on the stove in his apartment and transport it to the restaurant by subway. And it was better the next day anyway. Roasted meat was relatively easy—the pizza oven was always hot. For a long time, that's where pork chops got finished after a sear on the camping stove. Carlo made fluke crudo in the summer because it didn't require anything but a knife. He also started making pici from scratch, rolling it out on a picnic table outside because there wasn't enough prep space in the kitchen. When the garden got on its feet, he used what he could from there.

GOLDEN TILEFISH

egg yolk, chanterelle, caviar

4 (170- to 227-gram/
  6- to 8-ounce) golden
  tilefish fillets,* skin and
  scales on

Kosher salt

4 large egg yolks

White balsamic vinegar

Some good olive oil

100 grams (3½ ounces)
  chanterelle mushrooms,
  cleaned

Sherry vinegar

Unsalted butter

15 grams (½ ounce)
  caviar, preferably
  American hackleback
  (otherwise whatever
  you like and can afford)

Golden tilefish has a nice mellow flavor. The important word there is *flavor*. It has more flavor than your average whitefish, so it can handle the richness of mushrooms and eggs. As for the mushroom and the egg, they give this dish a strange and amazing surf-and-turf quality that gets us every time.

Preheat the oven to 325°F. Bring the fish to room temperature and salt it.

In a bowl, whisk the egg yolks together with a couple of splashes of white balsamic, a pinch of salt, and a small splash of warm water. Whisk very hard for a minute or two, and check the seasoning. The sauce should be egg-yolky with a hint of acid; it might need a little more salt.

Coat a large sauté pan with olive oil and set it over almost high heat. Cooking one fillet at a time, put the fish in the pan, skin side down, and keep your hand on it to keep it from buckling. After 1 to 1½ minutes, the fish should no longer be sticking to the pan and the skin should be crisp. Transfer the fish skin side up to a sheet pan and repeat with the remaining fillets. (Set the sauté pan aside.) Put the fillets in the oven and bake for 6 to 7 minutes. Check for doneness by inserting a metal skewer into one of the fillets. If the skewer comes out cold, let the fish cook for another minute. If it comes out warm, the fish is done.

In the meantime, coat another large sauté pan well with olive oil and set it over almost high heat. When the pan is hot, add the chanterelles. Cook them for 3 to 4 minutes, giving the pan a shake now and then; they should start to brown at the edges. Turn the heat off and season with salt and big splash of sherry vinegar.

Wipe out the large sauté pan you cooked the fish in, and put it back on the stove on medium heat. Add a big pat of butter to the pan, let it melt a little, and put the fillets, skin side down and two at a time, in the pan. Baste the fish with the butter for about a minute, taking the pan on and off the heat so the fish stays warm but doesn't continue to cook. Put the fish on four plates. Spoon a couple of spoonfuls of the egg yolk mixture over each fillet, and divide the mushrooms and the caviar among the plates. Serve.

* This is another tricky fish. Unlike golden tilefish from the Gulf of Mexico, golden tilefish from the mid-Atlantic has not been overfished and is not on any watch lists. At least it wasn't at the time that we wrote this book. The state of fish species changes all the time; you should find an online resource you trust and check it often if a fish's sustainability is important to you. If you need a substitute for tilefish for this recipe, try very fresh halibut.

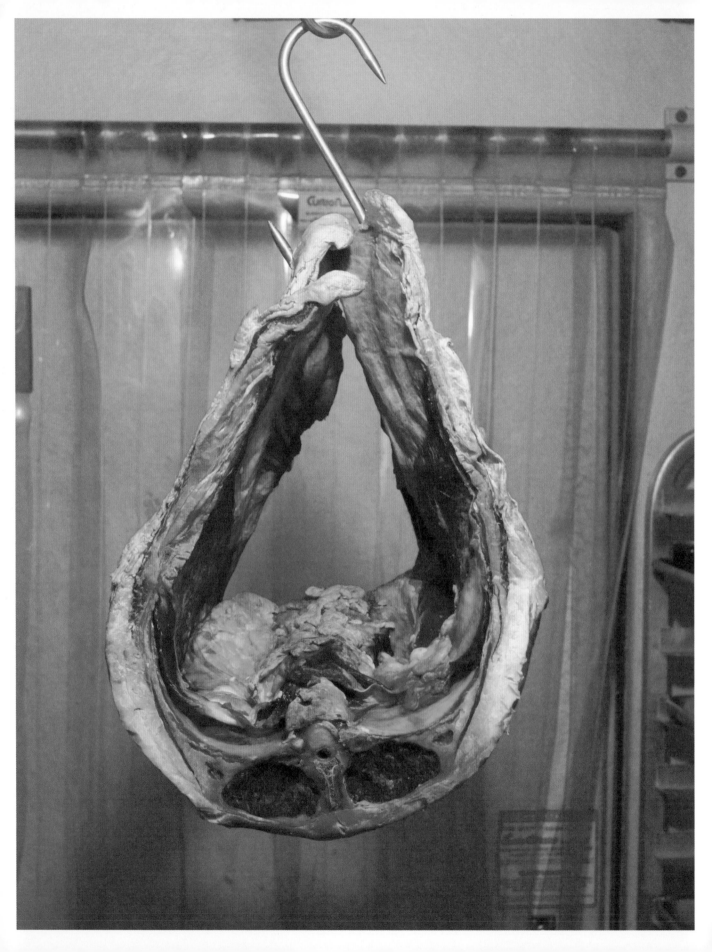

MEAT

We like meat that has flavor, and meat that tastes exactly like what it is, rather than also like some other things. For that reason, we like heritage breeds of pork. We like game birds and Hungarian pigs and chickens that get to eat bugs. We like beef aged long enough for its flavor to get deep and dark and funky.

Because we like those kinds of meats, we don't often come up against questions about an animal's origins or lifestyle or what kind of drugs it might have taken. We know where our meat comes from. Which is nice for us. We realize that it's not always possible to find or afford the kind of meat we deal with in this chapter. And we're not going to send you off with the advice to find a good butcher and ask him some questions. Good butchers, while they certainly exist, aren't coffee shops. That's true even in the artisanal-heirloom-heritage utopia that is our corner of the world.

If you have a good butcher near you, you should of course see if he has or can get what you need. If not, we've shared all of our sources. It might seem like a lot of hoops to jump through—tracking down a venison saddle, for instance. But in general, everybody eats too much meat, right? Us included. It just might be that the best way to rein in your meat consumption is to refuse to eat anything but the good stuff.

GUINEA HEN
wild rice, lacinato kale, heart and liver

SERVES 2 TO 4

50 grams (⅓ cup plus 2 teaspoons) kosher salt, plus more as needed

1 (1.1- to 1.4-kilogram/ 2½- to 3-pound) guinea hen*

Some good olive oil

2 parsnips, halved crosswise

2 medium turnips, halved

1 kohlrabi, halved

1 large onion, quartered

1 (4-inch) piece kombu (see note, page 188)

160 grams (1 cup) wild rice**

Freshly ground black pepper

1 large bunch lacinato kale (see note, page 55), ends trimmed

A pinch of chili flakes

White balsamic vinegar

Half a lemon

You don't see guinea hen on a lot of menus, let alone dinner tables, in America, but it's basically the pot roast of France. In fact it's popular all over Europe and elsewhere in the world. Guinea hens are beautiful feathered birds with big bodies and tiny heads. They like to roam, and anyone raising them has no choice but to let them do that. So while they don't come with "free range" labels, you can still be sure they got around. Which means the meat is dark, really flavorful, and just a little bit gamy. It doesn't taste like chicken. It tastes like guinea hen.

Combine 960 grams (4 cups) water and the salt in a pot and place it over high heat. Bring the liquid to a boil and when the salt dissolves, remove the pot from the heat and let the brine cool. Refrigerate until well chilled.

Remove the organs and neck from inside the cavity of the guinea hen, and set aside the heart and liver. Rinse the bird and pat it dry. Put the brine and the bird in a container or large sealable plastic bag, making sure the bird is completely submerged. Refrigerate it for at least 12 and up to 24 hours.

Remove the guinea hen from the brine and pat it dry. Place it back in the refrigerator, uncovered, to let the skin dry completely, at least 3 hours and up to 8 hours.

About an hour before you want to put the bird in the oven, start the broth for the rice. Depending on the kind of wild rice you use, your cook time should be 45 minutes to 1½ hours. Coat the bottom of a large pot with olive oil and place it over medium heat. Add the parsnips, turnips, kohlrabi, and onion, and cook until they're just beginning to brown, about 10 minutes. Fill the pot three-quarters full with water and return it to the stove. Bring the water to a boil, and then lower the heat and let it simmer for 45 minutes.

Strain the broth through a fine-mesh sieve and return it to the pot. Add the kombu and turn the heat to medium. When the broth begins to simmer, remove the kombu and strain the broth again through a fine-mesh strainer. Return the broth to the pot and season it to taste with salt.

Put the rice in a saucepan with about 2 cups of the broth and set aside another cup (you'll have about 6 cups total; you can freeze the rest for soups and anything that calls for vegetable stock). Bring the broth to a boil and then lower the heat. Cover the pan and simmer for 45 minutes or longer, depending on the type of rice and the cooking instructions for it. You want the rice to have bite—don't overcook it. When it's done, remove it from the heat, uncover it, and fluff it with a fork.

Meanwhile, preheat the oven to 275°F. Remove the guinea hen from the refrigerator and let it come to room temperature.

Rub the guinea hen all over with olive oil and season it very generously with salt and pepper. Place it in a roasting pan, breast side down, and roast for 1 hour, until the bird is just turning golden. Remove it from the oven and let it rest at room temperature while you turn the oven up to 400°F. When the oven is at temperature, flip the bird over and roast it for another 10 to 15 minutes, until the skin is golden brown and starting to crisp and a thermometer inserted into the thigh registers 150°F. Remove it from the oven and let it rest for 25 to 30 minutes.

* You can order a whole guinea hen if you can't get one through a butcher (see sources, page 282).

** We use wild rice from a company called Bineshii in Michigan. It's harvested by canoe, according to Native American tradition, and it has great bite and incredible flavor. It just takes an extra long time to cook, about an hour to an hour and a half.

continues

Set the oven to 450°F. Break the guinea hen down, separating the breasts from the body and removing the legs, keeping the skin attached as much as possible and reserving the oysters (the two round morsels of dark meat up near the thigh). Put the pieces back in the roasting pan and return them to the oven for another 5 to 7 minutes, until the skin is well crisped. The meat will look pink, and even red closer to the bone. Remove the meat from the oven and season it with a little more salt and pepper. Break the breasts and legs into smaller pieces.

Coat a large sauté pan with oil and set it over medium-high heat. Add the kale with a splash of water, a big pinch of salt, and the pinch of chili flakes. Sauté it, turning it with tongs to coat it in oil, for 4 or 5 minutes, until it's wilted. Give the pan a big splash of white balsamic and a drizzle of olive oil, and check the seasoning.

Put the cooked rice in another large sauté pan along with some of its cooking liquid, a splash of the remaining vegetable broth, and a squeeze of lemon. Set the pan over medium heat and season the rice with salt and pepper to taste. Season the reserved guinea hen heart and liver with salt, and finely chop them. Stir a quarter of the chopped organs into the rice. Taste it. If you love the rich, funky flavor of the organs, add the rest. If you're on the fence, leave the rice as is and cook it until the organs turn brown and the liquid is nearly gone, about 5 minutes. Season with salt and pepper to taste.

To serve, put the meat, kale, and rice in three separate serving dishes, or divide a mix of guinea hen meat and skin among two to four plates and give each plate a generous helping of rice and kale.

POULET ROUGE
cabbage, turnip, black radish

Poulet Rouge has a pretentious-sounding name for a chicken, but that's just because it's a breed of chicken from France. A breed of chicken that has much more than its fair share of evenly distributed fat, which makes for really flavorful, really juicy meat that's especially good grilled. We get ours from a guy named Carlo in Brooklyn who transports them live from a farm in Pennsylvania and slaughters them on his premises, so they're as fresh as they could possibly be. He sells poultry to a lot of Chinese restaurants, many of which have a thing about wanting their chickens to have been slaughtered that day.

Fill a large pot with the water and add the salt and sugar. Place the pot over high heat and bring the liquid to a boil. Boil until the salt and sugar have dissolved, then remove from the heat and let cool. Refrigerate until well chilled.

Remove and discard the organs from the cavity of the bird. Rinse the bird, pat it dry, and put it in a container with the brine, weighting it down if necessary to make sure it's completely submerged. Refrigerate for 24 hours.

Preheat the oven to 450°F. Remove the bird from the brine, pat it very dry, and let it come to room temperature. Rub it all over with olive oil and season it very generously with salt and pepper. Put it breast side up in a roasting pan and roast in the oven for 25 to 30 minutes, until the skin is just starting to crisp and a thermometer inserted into the breast reads 108°F. Turn the oven up to 475°F for the turnips.

SERVES 2 TO 4

3½ kilograms (3¾ quarts) water

175 grams (generous ¾ cup) kosher salt, plus more as needed

110 grams (½ cup) sugar

1 (1.4- to 1.6-kilogram/ 3- to 3½-pound) Poulet Rouge*

Some good olive oil

Freshly ground black pepper

225 grams (8 ounces) Japanese turnips,** whole

2 black radishes

Half a lemon

Unsalted butter

1 head Savoy cabbage, cored and thinly sliced

10 grams (1½ teaspoons) maple syrup

White balsamic vinegar

continues

Prepare a charcoal grill for medium-high heat or light a gas grill. Remove the legs from the bird and put them skin side down on the direct-heat side of the grill. Grill, turning once, until the skin is golden brown and crisp, 6 to 8 minutes. Put the breast, still on the crown of the bird, skin side down on the grill and grill for 5 minutes, until the skin is golden brown and crisp. Remove the chicken pieces from the grill and let them rest for 5 minutes.

In the meantime, toss the turnips with a couple of splashes of olive oil and season with salt and pepper. Put them on a rimmed sheet pan and roast them for about 20 minutes, turning them halfway through, until golden brown.

Using a mandoline or a very sharp knife, slice the radishes paper thin. In a bowl, toss them with a little olive oil, a big squeeze of lemon juice, and salt and pepper. Set aside.

Put a couple of tablespoons of butter in large, deep sauté pan and set it over medium-high heat. When the butter is melted, add the cabbage, stirring it with a wooden spoon to coat. Sauté the cabbage until it's tender and just starting to color, about 5 minutes. Turn off the heat, drizzle the cabbage with the maple syrup, add a big splash of white balsamic and toss it gently. Season it with salt to taste. In a large bowl, gently toss the turnips and cabbage together. Check the seasoning and adjust if necessary.

To serve, pull each piece of meat into a few smaller pieces and divide them among two to four plates, making sure to include plenty of skin. Give each plate a helping of turnips and cabbage and scatter the radishes over them. Serve.

* Poulet Rouge are being raised in lots of places in the U.S. now. You're still not likely to find them at your local butcher or supermarket, but you can order them (see sources, page 282).

** Japanese turnips, or Tokyo turnips, are smaller and sweeter and more delicately flavored than the average turnip. If you can't find them, look for white turnips or Macombers, which are bigger but still sweet and mild.

BANE'S FRIED CHICKEN

We once had the luck to be a pit stop for Carolyn Bane, chef and co-owner of Pies 'n' Thighs, a killer Southern-style spot in Williamsburg. She was between locations of her restaurant and she bided her time in our kitchen, during which time she could have taken credit for half the traffic that came through the place, especially during brunch. Bane's fried chicken—crunchy, moist, as addictive as you can imagine if you haven't had it—is a fixture in Roberta's history, but the recipe is all hers.

Fill a large pot with the water and add the salt and sugar. Place the pot over high heat and bring the liquid to a boil. Boil until the salt and sugar have dissolved, then remove from the heat and let cool. Refrigerate until well chilled.

In a small bowl, combine the paprika, cayenne, and black pepper. Season the chicken pieces well with the spice mixture and add them to the chilled brine. Refrigerate for 24 hours.

Remove the chicken from the brine, rinse it, pat it dry, and let it come to room temperature. Fill a cast-iron skillet with 2 inches of canola oil, set it over medium-high heat, and heat it until a cooking thermometer registers 350°F.

Put the flour in a shallow baking dish. Dredge the chicken in the flour, shake off the excess, and add it to the oil in batches. Slide a fish spatula under the chicken pieces so they don't stick to the bottom of the pan. Cook the chicken until golden brown and crisp, 12 to 15 minutes. "When they float, they're done," in Bane's words. Transfer the chicken pieces to a paper-towel-lined plate, season with salt, and serve.

SERVES 4

- 3½ kilograms (3¾ quarts) water
- 175 grams (generous ¾ cup) kosher salt, plus more as needed
- 110 grams (½ cup) sugar
- 6 grams (1 tablespoon) paprika
- 5 grams (scant 2 teaspoons) cayenne
- 3.5 grams (1 teaspoon) freshly ground black pepper
- 8 boneless chicken thighs
- Canola oil
- 411 grams (about 3 cups) all-purpose flour

FOIE GRAS
almond milk, hidden rose apple, black pepper

SERVES 4

225 grams (1½ cups) blanched unsalted Marcona almonds

711 grams (3 cups) water

18 grams (1 tablespoon) honey

Kosher salt

Some good olive oil

4 (60-gram/2-ounce) portions duck foie gras

1 Hidden Rose apple,* or Pink Lady or Honeycrisp, cut into 8 wedges

Freshly ground black pepper

* Hidden Rose is a variety of apple that has pink flesh, which makes it a really pretty addition to a plate. Flavor- and texture-wise, it's not all that different from the crisp, sweet-tart suggested substitutions.

Duck foie gras from Hudson Valley Foie Gras is the only kind of foie gras we've ever served. The ducks there are specially bred for the production of foie gras and they have the run of a beautiful spot a couple of hours north of the city. We have served foie gras lots of different ways but this way is our favorite—not too fussy, but memorable.

In a large, dry sauté pan toast the almonds over medium heat for 30 seconds to a minute, until fragrant and just barely starting to color. In a bowl, combine the almonds with the water and let them soak overnight.

Put the soaked almonds, along with the soaking liquid, in a blender and blend until smooth, 2 to 3 minutes. Add the honey and a pinch of salt, and blend for a few seconds to combine. Strain the mixture through a fine-mesh strainer, pushing it with a spatula to extract the liquid from the remaining pulp. Discard the pulp left in the strainer. Stretch a big piece of cheesecloth over a bowl (secure it with large rubber bands) and pour the almond milk over it. Let the milk strain overnight.

Preheat the oven to 350°F. Coat a large oven-safe sauté pan with olive oil, and then dump out any excess oil; you want the pan to have just a sheen of oil. Set the pan over medium-high heat. Season the foie gras with salt and put it in the pan. Cook it for about 1 minute per side, until it's lightly crisp and golden brown. Use a spoon to baste the foie gras in a little of its cooking liquid, then transfer the pan to the oven for 3 to 4 minutes. Press on a piece of foie gras with your finger; it should be firm but with a little give. If it feels very firm, it's still raw on the inside.

Put a couple of spoonfuls of almond milk in each of four very shallow bowls. Place the foie gras on top, along with 2 apple wedges. Garnish each plate with a couple of grindings of black pepper, and serve.

LAMB BREAST
goat yogurt, black trumpet mushroom, spigarello

This dish is the happy ending to a lamb breast rags-to-riches story. Before the restaurant had gas—or heat, for that matter—Carlo did a lot of his cooking at home. If you live in New York City, it's possible you once saw a tired man sitting on the subway with a sheet pan that reeked of meat on his lap. That was him.

Carlo cooked lamb breast low and slow all night at home and hauled it to the restaurant the next day. For service, he crisped portions of it in takeout containers in the toaster oven. The lamb breast at the restaurant is now a perfectly symmetrical, tender little package that's actually two lamb breasts stuck together with meat glue, pressed, and cooked sous vide. The old lamb and the new lamb are both winners. The recipe here is a refined version of the old lamb—it's more easily done at home and, if need be, portable.

Preheat the oven to 350°F. To prepare the herb paste, combine the garlic, kosher salt, rosemary, mint, maple sugar, and several grinds of black pepper in a blender. Add the olive oil and puree for about 1 minute, until the mixture has the consistency of a thick paste.

Cover the meat of the lamb breast thoroughly with the paste and place it, ribs side down, in a roasting pan that's just big enough to hold it. Cover the pan tightly with foil and roast for 2 to 3 hours, until a thermometer inserted in the meat reads 170°F. (The cooking time will depend on the size of the lamb breast and the calibration of the oven.) Remove the lamb from the oven and let it cool. Refrigerate it overnight.

When you're ready to finish cooking the lamb, take it out of the refrigerator and cut the breast and ribs from the bone. Separate the ribs and

SERVES 4 TO 6

FOR THE HERB PASTE

4 garlic cloves, peeled

14 grams (1½ tablespoons) kosher salt

5 sprigs rosemary, leaves picked

5 sprigs mint, leaves picked

10 grams (1 tablespoon) maple sugar*

Freshly ground black pepper

60 grams (generous ¼ cup) good olive oil

1 (about 1.3-kilogram/ 3-pound) bone-in lamb breast (see note, page 145)

1 lemon

225 grams (1 cup) goat's milk yogurt

Some good olive oil

continues

A small handful of mint leaves, finely chopped

Kosher salt

Freshly ground black pepper

340 grams (12 ounces) trumpet mushrooms, or maitake or chanterelle mushrooms, cleaned

Sherry vinegar

Sea salt, preferably Maldon

1 garlic clove, peeled

A pinch of chili flakes

2 to 3 bunches spigarello,** thick ends trimmed

* Maple sugar is nice for baking but it's incredible with meat. If you can't find it, you can substitute brown sugar here; just use an additional ½ tablespoon of it.

cut the breast into slabs about ½ inch thick. Let the meat come to room temperature.

Grate the zest of the lemon (set the lemon aside; you'll need it later). Whisk the yogurt together with a splash of olive oil, the lemon zest, the mint, a good pinch of kosher salt, and a few grinds of black pepper. Taste and adjust the seasoning if necessary.

Prepare a grill for medium-high heat or place a large sauté pan over medium-high heat. In batches, brown the lamb pieces for a few minutes on each side, until brown and crispy all over. Set aside to rest.

Generously coat a large sauté pan with olive oil and place it over medium-high heat. When the oil is hot, put the mushrooms in the pan with a pinch of kosher salt and let them brown for 2 to 3 minutes without moving them. Turn them over and let them brown another 2 to 3 minutes. Turn off the heat and give the pan a splash of sherry vinegar. Sprinkle the mushrooms with a little sea salt and transfer to a plate.

Wipe out the sauté pan, coat it well with olive oil, and place it over medium-high heat. Smash the garlic clove and add it to the pan with the pinch of chili flakes. Put the spigarello in the pan with a pinch of kosher salt. Sauté it for 5 to 6 minutes, turning it with tongs to toss it in the oil. Turn off the heat and give the pan a big squeeze of lemon juice.

Serve everything on platters or divide the meat, mushrooms, and spigarello among four to six plates and give each plate a big spoonful of yogurt sauce.

** This is an Italian heirloom variety of broccoli that's leafier and more delicate than broccoli rabe, and also sweeter and a little less bitter. If you can find it at the farmers' market, try it. If you can't, you can substitute broccoli rabe.

SPLIT PEA SOUP WITH BENTON'S BACON

The secret ingredient in this soup should be obvious. It ain't the split peas. You could make a case that Miller High Life is the secret ingredient, but you'd be wrong. Benton's bacon, cured and smoked by Allan Benton and company in the hills of Tennessee, is the most deeply flavorful, deeply smoky bacon we've ever had and probably ever will have. It's the muscle in this soup, which is thick and hearty and powerful enough to knock the winter doldrums unconscious.

Put the split peas in a strainer and rinse them very thoroughly with cold water. Set a large heavy-bottomed pot over medium-low heat and add the bacon. Sweat the bacon slowly until it begins to soften, 5 to 10 minutes. Add the carrot and onion to the pot and cook until they soften and the onion is translucent, 5 to 7 minutes.

Add the split peas and water to cover (about 2½ cups). Add the beer to the pot along with a couple of pinches of salt and a few grindings of black pepper. Bring to a simmer, cover, and let cook on a very gentle simmer for 2 hours, stirring regularly and adding water as needed to keep the peas covered. The consistency should be like a thick puree. If it's not, continue cooking and stirring. It's not possible to overcook this soup. When it's done, check the seasoning and serve.

SERVES 6

- 340 grams (1⅔ cups) green split peas

- 6 slices (about 240 grams/ 8 ounces) Benton's bacon, diced

- 1 large carrot, finely chopped

- 1 medium onion, finely chopped

- 1 (12-ounce) can Miller High Life or any lager

- Kosher salt

- Freshly ground black pepper

We were always into food. You'd think that would go without saying, but now that we think about it, maybe it doesn't. We weren't restaurant people. We weren't making jam or writing food blogs or collecting cookbooks. But we'd grown up in families that appreciated good food when all that meant was that you cared about quality ingredients, seasonality, where and how something was grown. We hosted dinner parties at our houses. We bought stuff at farmers' markets.

So when we planted some tomatoes and peppers in a planter we'd made out of the last of those shitty bricks, it wasn't some grand or even thoughtful gesture. It made sense to us that if we had the space and the sun—and because of all the low-slung buildings around us, we had a shitload of sun, like an amount of sun that usually only comes with real estate for rich people—we would grow something.

Somewhere in the early part of our second year, when things were about as full-tilt as ever, our friend Patrick Martins, the owner of Heritage Foods USA, approached us about doing a radio station in our backyard. Then things just came together and started happening the way they always did then, and the way we like to think they still do. Someone knew someone who could get a shipping container from the port in Elizabeth, New Jersey. We got that in and went to work building it out so Patrick could use it to start Heritage Radio. When we were done with it, it looked like a woodshed where commies would hide out. But it worked— apart from being so fucking freezing back there in the winter that it's amazing there was never a death by space heater.

VENISON SADDLE
sunchoke, pomegranate, chestnut

225 grams (8 ounces) duck fat (see note, page 148)

8 to 10 shelled chestnuts

1 (2.3- to 2.7-kilogram/ 5- to 6-pound) venison saddle, on the bone,* trimmed

Some good olive oil

Kosher salt

Freshly ground black pepper

4 sprigs thyme

4 sprigs sage

2 bay leaves

5 grams (1 teaspoon) dried juniper berries

454 grams (1 pound) sunchokes (also called Jerusalem artichokes), washed and sliced ¼ inch thick

1 pomegranate

There are rules about how venison gets to the table at restaurants. You can't just shoot a deer and serve it up. We get ours from one of a few game ranches in Texas. Deer and other animals live there a lot like how they would in the wild, and then they're hunted and slaughtered according to USDA standards. There are farm-raised versions of these animals but the meat isn't nearly as flavorful. Venison is beautiful meat, deep red in color with a clean, meaty flavor. The only way you can do wrong by it is to overcook it or bathe it in a bunch of fat or braising liquid. Just because it's lean meat doesn't mean it needs a lot of doctoring. Cook it until it's just rare. You'll understand what we mean.

Preheat the oven to 275°F. In a saucepan over medium-low heat, melt the duck fat. Put the chestnuts in a baking dish that's just big enough to fit them, and pour the duck fat over them. Bake for 1½ hours, until you can easily pierce a chestnut with the tip of a sharp knife. Remove from the oven and let cool. Take the chestnuts out of the duck fat, dry them off, and slice them into ¼-inch slices. Set the chestnuts aside. (You can reuse the duck fat if you add a pinch of salt to it and refrigerate it; it will keep for up to a month.)

Meanwhile, bring the venison to room temperature. Rub the meat with olive oil and season it generously with salt and pepper. Put it into a large roasting pan and scatter the thyme, sage, bay leaves, and juniper berries over it. Roast for 55 to 65 minutes, depending on the size of the saddle; 8 to 10 minutes per pound will get the meat to rare. Press on the meat with your finger; it should have some give. Remove the saddle from the oven and cover it loosely with foil. Let it rest at least 20 minutes.

Increase the oven temperature to 425°F. Toss the sunchokes with a couple of splashes of olive oil and season them with salt. Roast them on a sheet pan until they begin to caramelize and brown at the edges and the flesh is tender but firm, 15 to 20 minutes.

In the meantime, halve the pomegranate and submerge the halves in a bowl of water. Using your fingers, separate the seeds from the flesh. Set aside half of the seeds. Put the other half of the seeds in a mesh strainer set over a bowl and press them with the back of a big spoon to extract the juice. Discard the seeds in the strainer.

To serve, slice the venison into pieces about an inch thick, figuring 1 to 2 slices per person. Arrange the slices on a platter, and drizzle with the pomegranate juice and sprinkle with the reserved pomegranate seeds. Arrange the sliced chestnuts around the meat and serve with the roasted sunchokes on the side.

* Since it's unlikely you have a hookup at a game ranch, a good butcher is probably your best bet. If they don't carry venison saddle, also called loin, they might be able to get it for you. Otherwise, you can order it online.

PORCHETTA

4 garlic cloves, peeled

Some good olive oil

5 sprigs sage

5 sprigs rosemary

210 grams (1 cup plus
1½ tablespoons)
kosher salt

Grated zest of 1 lemon

5 grams (1 teaspoon)
fennel pollen*

5 grams (1 teaspoon)
fennel seeds

Freshly ground black
pepper

1 (2.3- to 2.7-kilogram/
5- to 6-pound) pork
belly, skin on

3.8 kilograms (4 quarts)
water

1 (1.4- to 1.6-kilogram/
3- to 3½-pound) pork
collar**

There are probably as many recipes for porchetta in Italy as there are Italian grandmothers. Everyone does her (or his) slow-roasted pork a little differently. We do ours by wrapping pork collar, a fatty cut that runs from the pig's neck to the loin, in pork belly. The layer of belly keeps the collar from drying out. It is a process. But the result is so good it will obliterate your memory of the process.

Put the garlic cloves in a small saucepan and pour about an inch of olive oil into the pan, enough to cover them completely. Put the saucepan over medium-low heat and cook for 1 hour, being careful not to let the garlic brown. Remove the garlic from the oil and set it aside to cool. (Strain the oil into a glass container and store it in the refrigerator. It will have a mild garlic flavor; you can use it for sautéing and in dressings.)

Pick the leaves of 3 of the sage sprigs and 3 of the rosemary sprigs. In a bowl, combine the leaves with 1½ tablespoons of salt, the lemon zest, fennel pollen, fennel seeds, confit garlic, and 7 or 8 grinds of black pepper. Transfer the pork belly to a container and rub it all over with the salt mixture. Cover and and refrigerate for 24 hours.

In a large pot, combine 1 cup of salt with the water and the remaining sage and rosemary. Place the pot over high heat and bring the liquid to a boil. Boil until the salt has dissolved, then remove from the heat and let cool. Refrigerate until very cold (at least a few hours and ideally overnight). Submerge the pork collar in the brine, cover, and refrigerate for 24 hours.

Remove the pork collar from the brine and wipe it off. Wipe the excess cure off the belly. Let both pieces of meat come to room temperature.

Preheat the oven to 350°F. Lay the collar on top of the flesh side of the belly. Fold the belly over the collar, and using kitchen twine, tie the two pieces of meat together at the ends and in the middle. Trim off and discard the excess belly and place the meat in a roasting pan.

Roast for 50 minutes, and then increase the oven temperature to 400°F and roast for another 15 minutes, until the skin is crispy and a meat thermometer inserted into the collar reads 120°F. Remove from the oven and let the meat rest for at least 20 minutes. Cut it into 1-inch-thick slices and serve.

* Fennel pollen has become a sort of cult ingredient in recent years, but it's been used in northern Italian cooking for centuries. A powder made from the buds of flowering fennel plants, it has potent fennel flavor but also a slight sweetness that enhances the flavor of whatever it's added to or rubbed into—especially pork. You can get it at gourmet food shops and online, easily.

** Pork collar is a fatty, flavorful cut from the part of the pig's shoulder that runs from the base of the neck to the top of the loin; it's becoming more popular but it's still not the easiest cut to find. Go to the best butcher or supermarket meat counter you can find and ask for it; you may have to special order it. And if the butcher can't or won't get collar for you, you can ask for the shoulder end of the loin instead.

DOUBLE-CUT COUNTRY RIB CHOP

SERVES 2

---

68 grams (½ cup) kosher
   salt, plus more as
   needed

4 sprigs rosemary, leaves
   of 1 sprig picked and
   finely chopped

1.8 kilograms (2 quarts) of
   water

2 (about 680-gram/
   1½-pound) double-cut
   1½- to 2-inch-thick
   country rib pork chops*

   Canola oil

30 grams (2 tablespoons)
   unsalted butter

1 sprig thyme, leaves
   picked and finely
   chopped

* Any time you have the ability
and money to buy pork from
a heritage breed, do it. The
animal will have been raised
humanely and the meat will be
more flavorful than commercial
pork. Our original rib chops
came from Red Wattle pigs,
courtesy of Heritage Foods.

Patrick Martins is the founder of Heritage Foods USA, which sells meat from sustainably raised, heritage-breed animals. Long before he moved his radio station into a shipping container in our backyard, he was our pork dealer. We'd been doing a pork loin chop as a kitchen special when Patrick told us he had this other cut we might like called the country rib chop. It comes from the shoulder end of the loin. The muscle there doesn't work very hard, so the meat has more fat and porkier flavor than the loin. The way we cook chops at the restaurant is to sous vide them and finish them in the wood-fired oven. Sous vide doesn't just cook the meat evenly, it breaks down the fat on the chop and bastes the meat with it, so you end up with an extremely tender and flavorful piece of meat. That's the royal treatment. You can also just brine, sear, and finish the chops in a hot oven—it'll be hard to imagine they could be better.

In a pot, combine the salt and the 3 whole rosemary sprigs with the water. Bring the liquid to a boil, then let it cool slightly and strain it through a fine-mesh strainer. Refrigerate until very cold (at least a few hours and ideally overnight). Place the chops in the brine and refrigerate them for 12 hours.

When you're ready to cook the chops, remove them from the brine, dry them off, and let them come to room temperature.

To begin the chops sous vide, lightly salt them on both sides. Place the chops in a sous-vide bag and vacuum-seal the bag. Cook at 64°C/147°F for 25 minutes; the meat will be almost done, but not quite. Remove the chops from the bag, dry them off, and let them rest for 20 minutes.

Coat a large sauté pan or a cast-iron skillet with canola oil and place it over almost high heat. Turn up the heat to high, add the chops, and season each with a little salt. Brown them for about 8 minutes, turning them occasionally, until the fat looks golden and caramelized.

Lower the heat as low as it goes, and add the butter and the chopped rosemary and thyme to the pan. Baste the chops in the melted butter for a couple of minutes, remove them from the pan, and let them rest for 20 minutes. Serve.

To begin the chops on the stovetop, preheat the oven to 350°F. Coat a large sauté pan or a cast-iron skillet with canola oil and place it over almost high heat. Salt the chops lightly on both sides and add them to the pan. Brown them for about 10 minutes total, turning them occasionally, until the fat looks golden and caramelized.

Lower the heat as low as it goes, and add the butter and chopped herbs to the pan. Baste the chops in the melted butter for a couple of minutes, then transfer them to a cool pan and place them in the oven. Let them cook for another 25 to 30 minutes, until they're well caramelized and a metal probe inserted into the meat comes out warm, not cool. Remove from the oven and let them rest for 20 minutes. Serve.

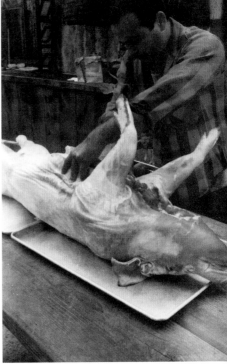

PORK COLLAR

applesauce, chrysanthemum greens, romanesco

SERVES 6 TO 8

6 Honeycrisp or Gala apples, cored and quartered

1 Granny Smith apple, cored and quartered

Kosher salt

Freshly ground black pepper

1 (2- to 2.3-kilogram/ 4½- to 5-pound) pork collar, preferably Mangalitsa*

Canola oil

1 head romanesco,** cut into florets

Unsalted butter

Some good olive oil

White balsamic vinegar

2 bunches chrysanthemum greens***

Half a lemon

Pork collar used to be an underrated cut but it's starting to catch on. Probably because it has plenty of fat, which means it's flavorful and almost never dry. The collar we use comes from Mangalitsa pigs raised in New Jersey at a place called Mosefund Farm. Mangalitsa is a Hungarian breed of pig that packs a tremendous amount of fat. The difference between Mangalitsa and any other pork collar is like the difference between Wagyu beef and regular beef. There's nothing sad about a tender, juicy regular pork collar. But if you're up for it, Mangalitsa is worth the splurge. The only problem is that you might never go back.

Put the apples in a large saucepan and cover with water. Set the pan over medium heat and bring to a simmer. Season with a big pinch of salt and several grindings of black pepper. Turn the heat down to medium-low, cover the pan, and simmer until the apples begin to break down, 10 to 15 minutes. Drain the fruit through a fine-mesh sieve set over a bowl to catch the cooking liquid. Put the fruit in a blender with ¼ cup of the cooking liquid, and puree until smooth. Check the seasoning—the applesauce should be tart and appley, not sweet.

Preheat the oven to 350°F. Slice the pork collar into 6 to 8 portions—a roughly 1½-inch-thick slice per serving. Salt and pepper each portion on both sides. Coat a large sauté pan or a cast-iron skillet with canola oil and set it over almost high heat. Sear the meat, in batches, for 6 to 7 minutes, turning occasionally. Transfer the seared meat to a sheet pan and put it in the oven for 4 to 6 minutes. The meat should be brown on the outside and pink on the inside; a metal probe inserted into it should come out warm, not cool. Let it rest for 20 minutes.

Meanwhile, put a big pot of salted water on to boil and prepare a bowl of ice water. Blanch the romanesco in the boiling water for 20 seconds, and plunge it into the ice water until cool. Drain well. Put a large sauté pan over medium heat and add a generous tablespoon of butter and a splash of olive oil to the pan. Add the romanesco to the pan and season it with salt and pepper. Sauté it for a couple of minutes, until it's tender but still has a bite. Give the pan a big splash of white balsamic and toss. Transfer the romanesco to a serving dish and wipe out the sauté pan. Coat the pan with olive oil and set it over medium-high heat. Add the chrysanthemum greens to the pan and season them with salt and pepper. Sauté the greens until they're wilted, 2 to 3 minutes. Give the pan a squeeze of lemon and check the seasoning.

To serve, divide the portions of pork among six to eight plates, and give each plate a big spoonful of applesauce and a serving of chrysanthemum greens and romanesco.

** Romanesco is an Italian variety of broccoli that's more cone-shaped than round and more chartreuse than green. It has a milder, sweeter flavor than regular broccoli. You can substitute broccoli or cauliflower here if you can't find it.

*** Chrysanthemum greens have a clean, grassy flavor and a bitter edge that softens when they're cooked. You can find them at Asian markets and some farmers' markets in the spring and fall. If you can't find them, you can substitute Swiss chard.

* You can order a whole Mangalitsa collar from Mosefund Farm: mosefund farm.com. If you're buying regular pork collar, go to the best butcher or supermarket meat counter you can find and ask for it. And if the butcher can't get collar for you, you can ask for the shoulder end of the loin instead. It won't be quite the same but it will still be good.

* Tripe isn't the easiest thing
to find. Ask for it at Asian or
South American markets, or see
if a butcher can get it for you.

** Lovage is like really, really
strongly flavored parsley. We
grow it in our garden. You can
find it at farmers' markets in
the spring and fall. If you can't,
substitute parsley.

TRIPE

serrano pepper, cider vinegar, lovage

Tripe is pretty unlovable-looking on a plate. And, being part of the stomach of a cow, it's unlovable on the fork to a lot of people too. But it's been surprisingly well loved at our restaurant. Maybe everybody comes primed for adventure. Maybe they're drunk when they order. In any case, this isn't exactly tripe for beginners, but it is a nice balance of warmth, heat, and acidity, which we think makes it approachable.

Bring a large pot of heavily salted water to a boil and prepare an ice bath. Blanch the tripe in the boiling water for 30 seconds to 1 minute, and transfer it to the ice bath with tongs, reserving the blanching liquid. Then dry it off and use a knife to scrape off the excess fat. Wrap the tripe in plastic wrap and transfer it to the freezer. Freeze for at least 2 hours.

Remove the tripe from the freezer and slice it into 1-inch-wide strips. In a large pot, combine the tripe with the wine, onion, carrot, celery, and enough of the reserved blanching liquid to cover the tripe by 2 inches. Set the pot over medium-high heat. Bring the liquid almost to a boil, and then reduce the heat to medium-low and simmer, covered, for 3 to 4 hours, until the tripe is softer but still somewhat firm.

Put a large saucepan over medium heat and add the butter. Add the tripe and a ladle or two of its cooking liquid. Add the serranos, a big splash of cider vinegar, and a couple of squeezes of lemon. Check the seasoning. Stir in the lovage leaves. Divide the tripe among four to six shallow bowls, garnish with a grind of black pepper, and serve.

SERVES 4 TO 6

---

907 grams (2 pounds) tripe,* well rinsed

225 grams (1 cup) dry white wine

1 onion, coarsely chopped

1 carrot, coarsely chopped

1 celery rib, coarsely chopped

35 grams (2 generous tablespoons) butter

2 serrano chilies, cored, seeded, and finely sliced

Cider vinegar

Half a lemon

A big handful of lovage,** leaves picked

Freshly ground black pepper

MARROW BONES

sea beans, grilled bread

SERVES 4 TO 6

---

12 (3- to 5-inch-long) center-cut veal marrow bones (about 1.5 kilograms/ 3½ pounds total)

Ice-cold, salted water

Kosher salt

Crusty bread

A big handful of sea beans (see note, page 175)

Some good olive oil

Half a lemon

Freshly ground black pepper

We are not alone in our love for marrow bones. But we roast them at a lower temperature than you might see suggested elsewhere. If you cook them at too high a temperature, the marrow can liquefy. At a lower temperature, it stays beautifully gelatinous.

Rinse the bones well. Put them in a container with enough ice-cold, salted water (it should be salted like you would pasta water) to cover them, and refrigerate them for 24 hours.

Preheat the oven to 350°F. Pull the bones from the water and dry them. Season them well with salt.

Put the bones on a foil-lined rimmed sheet pan and put them in the oven. Roast them for 15 to 20 minutes, until the marrow looks like it's setting. Insert a metal skewer into the marrow; if it comes out warm, the bones are done.

Slice the bread into thick slices and grill or broil it until it's brown at the edges.

In a bowl, toss the sea beans with a splash of olive oil, a big squeeze of lemon juice, and salt and pepper.

Give the bones a sprinkle of salt, and serve them with the dressed sea beans and grilled bread.

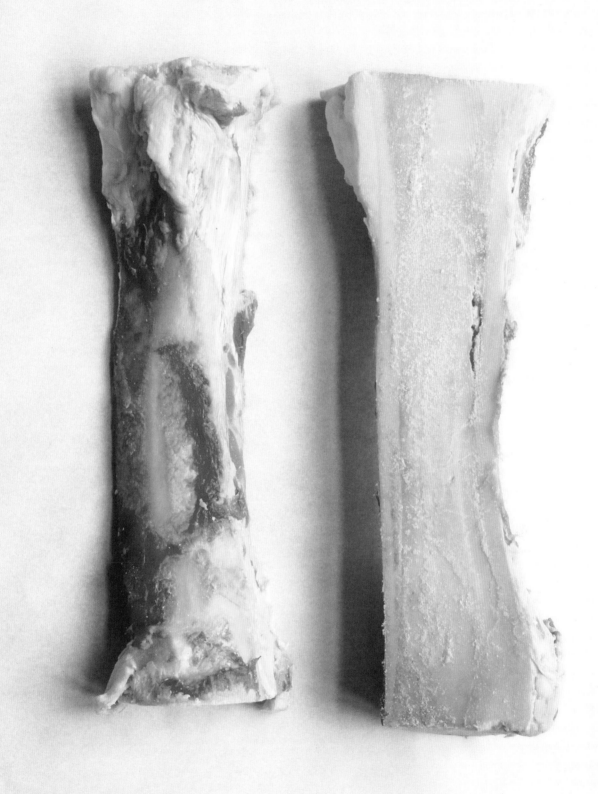

It was summer when we finished the inside of the shipping container. We looked at the roof of it and we looked at the sun and we went looking for some lumber. The plan was to build a greenhouse on top. Rooftop gardens weren't the seasonal cocktails of restaurants yet. We didn't know anyone who had one. To us, it just seemed like a wise use of space.

So we got the lumber and then looked into buying topsoil, which, it turns out, is fucking expensive. And as well as the restaurant was doing at that point, we weren't exactly sleeping on piles of cash. So we did some math. If we had a party and charged people an entry fee, we could raise enough to pay for the topsoil. Our landlords were never around on Fridays or Saturdays. We figured we could put the soil on a credit card, get it in on Friday afternoon, have the party Satur-

day, and have the whole place cleaned up by the time they came back around on Sunday.

The topsoil came by truck the next day. We had it dumped in the backyard and spread it out so we had several inches of cover. Then we built a dirt-bike track with our neighbors. It had an eight-foot-high jump that nine out of ten people couldn't or wouldn't go fast enough to clear. Lots of people hurt themselves a little. Some a lot. Everyone who came to the party had to sign a handwritten waiver saying: I'm a fucking adult and I know I might hurt myself. By the end of the night, someone had lost all the waivers. The whole thing was pretty magical.

BEEF CARPACCIO

caviar, watercress, gooseberry

SERVES 6 TO 8

1 (450-gram/1-pound) tri-tip steak, trimmed

Kosher salt

Freshly ground black pepper

Some good olive oil

Half a lemon

30 grams (1 ounce) caviar, preferably American hackleback (otherwise whatever you like and can afford)

A small handful of ripe gooseberries, halved*

A handful of watercress

* Gooseberries are around for just a few weeks in early to mid summer. You can use any color—pink, green, yellow— you can find, but the green ones have a tartness that works well here. You can get them at farmers' markets in season or frozen online.

We use Wagyu tri-tip from Kansas for carpaccio. Which sounds really cowboy-hat western for what ends up being a beautiful and delicate-looking dish. We use it because it's some of the most richly flavored beef around. But you can use any prime beef for this dish, so long as it's tri-tip. Tri-tip, cut from the bottom sirloin, is on the lean side but it has really nice beefy flavor.

Trim any remaining excess tissue from the steak, wrap it in plastic wrap, and freeze it for at least 8 hours and up to 12 hours. Remove it from the freezer and let it sit at room temperature for 30 minutes. Using a very sharp knife, slice the beef into slices as close to paper-thin as you can get; not quite paper-thin is okay. Put the beef on a platter or divide it among six to eight large plates, and let it come to room temperature.

Season the beef well with salt and pepper, and drizzle a generous amount of olive oil over it. Give the whole platter a squeeze of lemon. Put fingerfuls of caviar all around the platter and scatter the gooseberries over it. In a bowl, dress the watercress with a splash of olive oil, a squeeze of lemon, and salt and pepper. Scatter the watercress over the platter and serve.

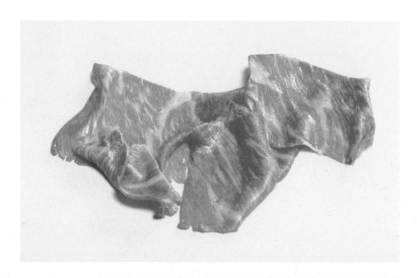

CHEESEBURGER

We put a burger on the menu because we wanted to eat one. That's the truth. But our burger wouldn't be in this book if it weren't awesome in the original sense of the word. The recipe is simple, but it begins with a not very accessible ingredient: a custom blend of dry-aged beef. It gives our burger an intense flavor that's hard to replicate at home. But what you can do is buy the best ground beef you can—there are other dry-aged ground beef blends out there—and follow these simple instructions.

Preheat the oven to 350°F. Let the beef come to room temperature, and season it very generously with salt and pepper. Form the beef into 4 loose patties—don't handle it too much or pack the patties too tightly—and season them.

Put a few drops of canola oil in a large ovenproof sauté pan or cast-iron pan, wipe the pan out with a paper towel, and set it over medium-high heat. Cook the burgers for 4 to 5 minutes total, flipping them once or twice. Put a slice of cheese on each burger, transfer them to a cool pan, and put them in the oven for 3 to 4 minutes. Press on the burger with your finger to check for doneness—for medium-rare, the meat should have a good amount of give, but not too much. Remove from the oven and let rest at least 5 minutes.

To serve, put each burger on the bottom half of a potato roll. Lay a romaine leaf and a slice of onion on the other half of the potato roll. Serve with ketchup on the side.

SERVES 4

680 grams (1½ pounds) ground beef, preferably dry-aged and 20 percent fat

Kosher salt

Freshly ground black pepper

Canola oil

4 slices American cheese, such as Land O'Lakes

4 potato rolls, homemade or store-bought, halved

4 crisp romaine leaves, cold

Half a white onion, thinly sliced

Ketchup

SKIRT STEAK
fingerlings, salsa verde, greens

This steak was one of the earliest additions to the menu when we started going beyond pizza, salad, and meat and cheese. We figured a real restaurant should have steak. And this one is a people's steak. We could afford it, people could afford it, and as far as we're concerned, a perfectly cooked skirt steak beats an okay rib eye any day.

In a bowl, combine the grapeseed oil, thyme, rosemary, the chopped garlic, and the habanero. Rub the mixture all over the skirt steak, transfer it to a container, cover it, and refrigerate it overnight.

When you're ready to cook the steak, remove it from the refrigerator, wipe off the excess marinade, and let it come to room temperature.

Preheat the oven to 275°F.

Put the potatoes in a large pot and cover them with water. Bring the water to a boil, reduce the heat slightly, and cook until the potatoes are just tender, 8 to 10 minutes. Drain the potatoes, pat them dry, and chill them in the refrigerator for at least 20 minutes.

Season both sides of the steak generously with salt and pepper. Put a small splash of grapeseed oil in a large ovenproof sauté pan or cast-iron skillet, and wipe the pan out with a paper towel. Set the pan over almost high heat. When the pan is hot, add the skirt steak and cook for about 2 minutes per side, until it's nicely seared all over. Transfer the steak to the oven and cook for another 2 to 3 minutes, until medium-rare. The meat should be brown on the outside and dark red on the inside, and a metal probe inserted into the thickest part of the steak should come out warm, not cool. Remove it from the oven and let it rest for 20 minutes.

SERVES 6 TO 8

60 grams (¼ cup) grapeseed or canola oil, plus more for cooking the steak

2 sprigs thyme, leaves picked and finely chopped

2 sprigs rosemary, leaves picked and finely chopped

6 garlic cloves, peeled: 4 finely chopped, 2 left whole

1 habanero, cored, seeded, and finely chopped

907 grams (2 pounds) skirt steak, ½ to 1 inch thick

680 grams (1½ pounds) fingerling potatoes, scrubbed and cut in thirds

Kosher salt

Freshly ground black pepper

continues

Some good olive oil

Chili flakes

2 bunches Swiss chard, ends trimmed, ribs removed, and roughly chopped

Half a lemon

Salsa verde (recipe follows)

Coat a large sauté pan or cast-iron pan generously with olive oil and set it over medium-high heat. When the pan is hot, add the potatoes and cook them, tossing them occasionally, until they're lightly crisp and brown, about 10 minutes. Season them generously with salt and pepper.

Coat a large sauté pan with olive oil and set it over medium-high heat. Thinly slice the remaining 2 garlic cloves and add them to the pan along with a generous pinch of chili flakes. Cook for 30 seconds or so, until the garlic is fragrant and beginning to color. Add the Swiss chard to the pan along with a big splash of olive oil, season it with salt and pepper, and sauté, occasionally tossing it with tongs, for 4 or 5 minutes, until tender. Give the pan a big squeeze of lemon juice and check the seasoning.

To serve, thinly slice the steak against the grain and season again with a little more salt and pepper. Divide the sliced steak among six to eight plates and top it with a big spoonful of salsa verde. Give each plate a serving of potatoes and Swiss chard.

salsa verde

In a blender, combine the parsley, capers, and garlic and blend briefly to combine. Blending constantly, add most of the olive oil in a slow stream, stopping before you use all of it. Add a big squeeze of lemon, the pinch of chili flakes, a big pinch of salt, and several grindings of black pepper, and blend for 30 seconds. Check the seasoning and the thickness. If it's too thick, add the remaining olive oil.

MAKES ABOUT 160 GRAMS
(ABOUT ¾ CUP)

2 handfuls of parsley
leaves

50 grams (scant ⅓ cup)
capers, drained

1 garlic clove, peeled

65 to 95 grams (⅓ to
½ cup) good olive oil

Half a lemon

A pinch of chili flakes

Kosher salt

Freshly ground black
pepper

SWEETBREADS
lime aioli

We usually think of using Wondra for frying as cheating; it's the flour that gets caramel-colored and crisp, not whatever you've coated with it. But sweetbreads are one of a few exceptions. Here it works perfectly, making a crisp coating so light you can barely call it a coating. These sweetbreads have been compared to all kinds of things, but mostly Chicken McNuggets and popcorn shrimp. They are delicately crisp on the outside and tender and buttery on the inside. They have clung to the menu like a barnacle.

Prepare a large bowl of ice water. Put the sweetbreads in the ice water and refrigerate them for at least 8 and up to 12 hours, changing the water a couple of times.

Drain the sweetbreads and prepare an ice bath. Put the sweetbreads in a big pot filled three-quarters full with well-salted water. Add 3 of the lemon halves to the pot, bring the water to a boil, and then reduce the heat and simmer for 3 minutes. The sweetbreads should be starting to firm up. Drain them and transfer to them to the ice bath for at least 1 minute. Using a small knife, trim the membrane and excess fat from the sweetbreads, and then break them into pieces just bigger than bite-size.

Season the sweetbreads generously with salt and pepper. Put the Wondra in a shallow baking dish and season it with a little salt and pepper. Toss the sweetbreads in the Wondra until they're well coated. Coat a large sauté pan with olive oil and set it over medium-high heat. When the oil is hot, add the sweetbreads; you may need to do this in two batches to avoid crowding the pan. Let the sweetbreads cook for 2 to 3

SERVES 4 TO 6 AS A SNACK

454 grams (1 pound) veal sweetbreads, well rinsed*

2 lemons, halved

Kosher salt

Freshly ground black pepper

340 grams (1¼ cups) instant flour, such as Wondra

Some good olive oil

30 grams (2 tablespoons) unsalted butter

1 lime

Lime aioli (recipe follows)

* Ask at a good butcher or go to an online purveyor and look for veal sweetbreads—technically the thymus gland of a calf. Opt for humanely raised and antibiotic-free if it's available and make sure whatever you buy smells clean, like organ meat but nothing else.

minutes on one side, then flip them individually and cook on the other side for another 2 to 3 minutes, until they're golden brown all over. Add the butter to the pan and baste the sweetbreads in it briefly. Transfer them to a paper-towel-lined plate, and give them a big squeeze of lime juice and a few grindings of black pepper. Finely grate a little lime zest over the sweetbreads, and serve with the aioli on the side.

lime aioli

MAKES 280 GRAMS (ABOUT 1½ CUPS)

2 large room-temperature egg yolks

6 grams (1½ teaspoons) freshly squeezed lime juice, plus more as needed

2.5 grams (generous ½ teaspoon) Dijon mustard

300 grams (1½ cups) canola, safflower, or vegetable oil

1 garlic clove, peeled and minced

Grated zest of half a lime

Kosher salt

In a blender or using a whisk, combine the egg yolks with the lime juice and mustard until well combined. Add a few drops of the oil and blend or whisk to combine. Add the rest of the oil in a very slow dribble, blending or whisking constantly. When the mayo starts to look thick and shiny, stop adding oil. If you've added all the oil and it seems too thick, thin it out with a splash of water. Add the garlic, lime zest, and a generous pinch of salt, and blend just until combined. Check the seasoning, adding more salt or lime juice as needed. The aioli will keep in the refrigerator for up to five days.

DRY-AGED STRIP LOIN

How a steak is aged is almost more important than how you cook it. The real work—the tenderizing and the flavor development—happens in those 40, 50, or 60 days when the meat is hanging out in a climate-controlled environment, occasionally tended to by obsessive butchers. We buy our beef from ranches we trust, and we send it to a New York butcher to be aged for 60 days or longer. The beef at most steakhouses is aged somewhere between 30 and 40 days. You need a minimum of 30 days for the steak to start developing flavor. For potent flavor, you need at least 40 days. In our opinion, things don't get interesting until around 50 days. Some people think the flavor of a steak aged 60 or more days is a little too funky. Not us.

In any case, since you probably can't get your hands on a steak aged for two months, and since aging beef at home is neither practical nor something we want to be responsible for teaching you, we'll just recommend that you buy the longest aged, best quality strip loin you can afford. It won't be cheap. Share it with someone you like.

Preheat the oven to 275°F and let the steak come to room temperature. Salt it very generously on both sides.

Put the potatoes in a large pot and cover them with water. Bring the water to a boil, reduce the heat slightly, and cook until the potatoes are just tender, 8 to 10 minutes. Drain the potatoes, pat them dry, and chill them in the refrigerator for at least 20 minutes.

Bring a large pot of heavily salted water to a boil and prepare a large bowl of ice water. Blanch the spigarello in the boiling water for 30 seconds, and then drain it and shock it in the ice water. Drain well and set aside.

SERVES 2

1 (907- to 964-gram/ 32- to 34-ounce) dry-aged strip loin, 1½ inches thick

Kosher salt

227 grams (8 ounces) fingerling potatoes

1 bunch spigarello (see note, page 212), thick ends trimmed

Some good olive oil

1 garlic clove, peeled and smashed

Chili flakes

Freshly ground black pepper

Half a lemon

Canola oil

Unsalted butter

1 sprig thyme, leaves picked and finely chopped

Sea salt, preferably Maldon

continues

Coat a large sauté pan or cast-iron pan well with olive oil and set it over almost high heat. When the oil is shimmering, put the steak in the pan and place another heavy pan on top of it, or just use your hand to press on it firmly; the goal is an evenly browned crust. Cook the steak for about 5 minutes on each side, until it has a good crust all around. Transfer it to a cool sheet pan and put it in the oven for 12 to 15 minutes, until medium-rare. Insert a metal probe into the thickest part of the steak; if it comes out cold, cook the steak for another minute or two. If it's warm, the steak is done. Remove it from the oven and let it rest for 10 minutes.

Coat a large sauté pan with olive oil and add the smashed garlic clove and a pinch of chili flakes. Set the pan over medium-high heat. Add the spigarello and sauté it, tossing it occasionally with tongs, for 3 to 4 minutes. Season it with salt and pepper, and give it a big squeeze of lemon juice and a drizzle of olive oil. Discard the garlic clove.

Coat a large sauté pan or cast-iron pan generously with olive oil and set it over medium-high heat. When the pan is hot, add the potatoes and cook them, tossing them occasionally, until they're lightly crisp and brown, about 10 minutes. Season them generously with salt and pepper.

Coat a large sauté pan or cast-iron pan very lightly with canola oil and set it over almost high heat. When the oil is hot, add the steak to the pan. Add a generous tablespoon of butter and the thyme to the pan and cook the steak, basting it in the butter and thyme for 2 minutes total, turning it every 30 seconds or so. Transfer the steak to a cutting board and let it rest for 5 minutes. Slice it on the bias against the grain and divide it between two plates. Drizzle any juice left in the pan over the steak, and sprinkle with a little sea salt. Give each plate a share of spigarello and potatoes, and serve.

DESSERT

What restaurants call a "composed dessert" doesn't always translate well to home cooking. Because usually when you go to the trouble to make dessert, you've just made a meal too. You probably want to keep things simple. Well, what follows are recipes for our favorite desserts, and they are indeed multi-parters. Desserts at Roberta's almost always have a frozen element. That was one of our outstanding pastry chef Katy Peetz's early signatures. After a meal of mostly warm and savory, it's nice to have a spoonful of something that wakes you up. But no one's judging composition at home. If you're not up for making semifreddo and stewing quince, the gingerbread (page 250) is still really good with plain whipped cream. You can skip the granita and have parsley cake (page 254) for breakfast, warm with a little butter. But if you're feeling adventurous—and especially if someone else is making dinner—try one of these in all its composed glory. You'll steal the show.

GINGERBREAD

miticrema semifreddo, quince

SERVES 8 TO 10

5 grams (2 teaspoons) caraway seeds

2 grams (scant ¾ teaspoon) whole black peppercorns

4 grams (scant 2½ teaspoons) whole coriander seeds

3 grams (generous 1 teaspoon) dried juniper berries

60 grams (4¼ tablespoons) unsalted butter, plus more for the pan

60 grams (⅓ cup) crème fraîche (page 109)

2 large eggs

125 grams (¾ cup plus 2 tablespoons) all-purpose flour

10 grams (1 tablespoon plus 1 teaspoon) cornstarch

50 grams (½ cup plus 1 tablespoon) almond flour

2 grams (scant ½ teaspoon) baking soda

If there were a contest for the gingeriest gingerbread, this would win. It is deep and dark and mysterious and delicious. As good as it is on its own, it's even better with the creamy tang of miticrema and the sweet-tartness of quince.

In a dry sauté pan over medium-low heat, toast the caraway seeds, black peppercorns, coriander seeds, and juniper berries. After about a minute, when the spices are becoming very fragrant, remove the pan from the heat and let cool. Grind the spices well in a spice grinder or a clean coffee grinder and set aside.

Let the butter, crème fraîche, and eggs come to room temperature. Preheat the oven to 340°F. Butter a loaf pan and line it with a strip of parchment paper that covers the bottom and the short sides of the pan. Lightly butter the parchment paper.

In a large bowl, combine the flour, cornstarch, almond flour, baking soda, baking powder, celery salt, kosher salt, cinnamon, and the reserved spice mix. Set aside.

In another bowl, use a whisk to beat the molasses, butter, honey, vanilla extract, sugar, olive oil, crème fraîche, eggs, and grated ginger together until smooth. Set aside.

Add the wet mixture to the dry mixture in thirds, mixing with a wooden spoon just until incorporated with each addition. The ingredients should be well combined but there may be butter lumps in the mixture; that's okay. Don't overmix. Fold in the crystallized ginger.

Pour the batter into the loaf pan and bake for 50 minutes, rotating the pan halfway through. The gingerbread is done when a cake tester inserted into it comes out clean. Remove it from the oven and let it cool in the pan

To serve, slice the cake into squares and place a square of warm gingerbread on each plate. Place two spoonfuls of the quince on the plate next to the gingerbread, then place a big spoonful of the semi-freddo next to it.

* Peel the ginger with a spoon and then grate it on a coarse cheese grater directly into a bowl so you don't lose any of the juices.

1.5 grams (¼ teaspoon) baking powder

2 grams (½ teaspoon) celery salt

2 grams (generous ½ teaspoon) kosher salt

7 grams (1 generous tablespoon) ground cinnamon

60 grams (¼ cup plus ½ tablespoon) molasses

60 grams (⅓ cup) honey

5 grams (1 teaspoon) vanilla extract

60 grams (⅓ cup) packed dark brown sugar

60 grams (generous ¼ cup) good olive oil

140 grams (5 ounces) fresh ginger, peeled and finely grated* (about ¾ cup)

40 grams (2 tablespoons) chopped crystallized ginger

Miticrema semifreddo (recipe follows)

Poached quince (recipe follows)

miticrema semifreddo

MAKES 770 GRAMS
(1 QUART)

250 grams (generous 1 cup)
heavy cream

300 grams (10½ ounces)
miticrema cheese, at
room temperature*

6 large egg yolks, at
room temperature

160 grams (heaping ¾ cup)
sugar

* Miticrema is a dense, creamy
sheep's milk cheese from
Spain. It's salty, bitter, and a
little tangy, which balances
out the sweetness and spice
of the gingerbread. Think of it
as glorified cream cheese, but
better.

Using a hand mixer, whip the heavy cream just until it forms stiff peaks; it should be the texture of whipped cream. Cover and refrigerate it.

Using a hand mixer, whip the miticrema for a couple of minutes; it should get lighter and airier. Set it aside.

Using a hand mixer or a blender, blend the egg yolks together with the sugar until the mixture is very thick and turns a pale yellow color; this should take 3 to 5 minutes.

Transfer the egg mixture to a bowl and gently whisk in the whipped miticrema. Use a rubber spatula to fold in the whipped cream. Pour the contents into a glass or plastic container, cover, and freeze until frozen, at least 6 hours and ideally overnight.

poached quince

Have any leftovers with vanilla ice cream or with granola and yogurt for breakfast.

SERVES 8 TO 10

3 lemons

3 large quince (about 1.4 kilograms/ 3 pounds total)

Half a vanilla bean, split lengthwise, seeds scraped

140 grams (¾ cup) sugar, plus more as needed

Wash and peel 1 lemon and reserve the skin. Juice all 3 lemons and divide the juice between two large bowls. Add the lemon peel to one of those bowls.

Peel and quarter the quince and cut out the cores—just like you would quarter an apple—reserving the peels and cores. Cut the quarters into ½-inch dice. Quince oxidizes and turns brown very quickly, so transfer the cut quince immediately to the bowl of lemon juice only (not the one with the peel), and toss it to coat. Add the quince peels and cores to the bowl with the lemon peel (the skin and cores of the quince contain pectin, which will give the finished poached quince a nice jam-like texture). Pour the diced quince and lemon juice into a wide-bottomed saucepan—the wider the better because that will allow the quince to cook more evenly.

Strain the remaining bowl of lemon juice, reserving the juice and the solids separately. In a mortar and pestle, smash the vanilla bean seeds together with 45 grams (¼ cup) of the sugar to make vanilla sugar. Add this, along with the remaining sugar, 455 grams (2 cups) water, and the strained lemon juice to the saucepan. Wrap the reserved lemon peel and quince skins and cores in cheesecloth, tie it in a bundle, and add it to the saucepan. The quince pieces in the pan should be completely covered with water. If they're not, add a little more water (and a little more sugar: 2 parts water to 1 part sugar) to cover them. Cover the saucepan and cook the quince on a very low simmer for about 1 hour. Check on it occasionally. It should turn from pale yellow to deep pink and smell very fragrant. If the water cooks down and the quince is uncovered, add a little more water to cover it.

When you can easily insert a sharp knife into one of the quince pieces, remove the quince from the pot with a slotted spoon and let it cool. Turn the heat under the saucepan up to medium and let the rest of the liquid cook down until it's syrupy, 15 to 20 minutes. Strain the liquid through a fine-mesh sieve and combine it with the poached quince. Let cool. The poached quince in syrup will keep in an airtight container in the refrigerator for up to a week.

PARSLEY CAKE

caramel fennel gelato, lemon zest granita

150 grams (4 cups tightly packed, from about 5 large bunches) parsley leaves

30 grams (1 cup tightly packed, from 2 bunches) mint leaves

165 grams (¾ cup) good olive oil, plus more for the pan

290 grams (2 cups plus 1 tablespoon) all-purpose flour

15 grams (1 tablespoon plus 2 teaspoons) cornstarch

7 grams (2¼ teaspoons) kosher salt

8 grams (1½ teaspoons) baking powder

4 large eggs, at room temperature

330 grams (1⅔ cups) sugar

This cake was the result of a wish to make something green—a dessert that really tasted and looked like it came from the garden, not one just garnished with something from the garden. It's herbaceous and vegetal but sweet enough to be called cake. The caramel fennel gelato it goes with is intense in a good way and borderline savory, but be warned: We crank up the black garlic because it works with the cake and the granita. If you plan to eat the gelato all on its own—no cake—use a little less black garlic.

To make the herb-oil mixture, put a fourth of the parsley and mint in a strong blender, such as a Vitamix, or in a food processor, and blend it on low speed. Use a blender stick to help crush the herbs while the blade is spinning (or stop the machine from time to time to push the herbs back down toward the blade). Slowly increase the speed to medium (or a steady puree, in a food processor) and continue adding the rest of the herbs until you have added all of them. In a steady stream, add half of the olive oil. Mix on medium-low speed (or pulsing, if using a food processor) until all is combined. Add the remaining olive oil and blend for no longer than 10 seconds. The mixture will look loose and stringy. Scrape out the blender to get all of the parsley mixture, transfer it to a bowl, and refrigerate until ready to use.

In a bowl, combine the flour, cornstarch, salt, and baking powder and set aside.

In a stand mixer fitted with the paddle attachment, whip the eggs for about 30 seconds. Add the sugar and mix on high speed until the mixture is very thick and turns a pale yellow color, about 3 minutes. Turn the mixer speed down to low and add the herb-oil mixture. With

the machine still running, add the flour mixture and mix until just combined. Do not overmix. Pour the batter into a container and refrigerate it for at least 6 and up to 24 hours (the cake will turn out much greener than it would if you baked it right away).

When you're ready to bake, preheat the oven to 340°F and spray a sheet pan—ideally 13- x 18-inch but 11¾- x 16½-inch will work with a slightly longer baking time—with cooking spray to coat it. Line the bottom of the pan with parchment paper and lightly spray the paper. Pour the batter into the sheet pan and smooth out the top with a spatula. Bake for 12 to 18 minutes, rotating the cake halfway through. If the top begins to brown before the inside of the cake is done, turn the heat down to 330°F and let it cook a couple of minutes longer. When a cake tester inserted in the center of the cake comes out clean, it's done. Let it cool in the pan.

To serve, tear serving-size squares of cake into a few larger pieces and divide them among individual plates. Put a scoop of caramel fennel gelato on each plate and scatter a smaller scoop of lemon zest granita over the cake and gelato. Scatter parsley cake crumble lightly over the gelato and granita, and serve.

Cooking spray

Caramel fennel gelato
(recipe follows)

Lemon zest granita
(recipe follows)

Parsley cake crumble
(recipe follows)

caramel fennel gelato

MAKES 1.15 KILOGRAMS
(1½ QUARTS)

940 grams (about 1 quart) whole milk

7 grams (2 teaspoons) fennel seeds, toasted

5 grams (2 to 3 cloves) black garlic (see note, page 178)

Grated zest of half a lemon, plus the juice as needed

37 grams (scant 2 tablespoons) maple syrup

200 grams (1 cup) sugar

332 grams (scant 1½ cups) heavy cream

100 grams (¾ cup) powdered milk

3 grams (generous ½ teaspoon) xanthan gum*

4 grams (½ teaspoon) kosher salt

2 large eggs, at room temperature

In a blender, combine the milk, toasted fennel seeds, black garlic, lemon zest, and maple syrup. Blend on medium speed until well combined. Pour the mixture into a saucepan and set it over medium heat. Bring to a simmer, then turn the heat to low and cover. Let steep for 1 hour, checking to make sure the liquid isn't simmering (if it is, turn the heat as low as possible or move the pan to a smaller burner). Let it cool, transfer it to a container, and refrigerate it overnight. The next day, strain the liquid through a fine-mesh sieve and refrigerate until ready to use.

In a very large pot (extra-large because you'll be making a caramel, which bubbles up high), combine the sugar with a few splashes of tepid water and set it over medium heat. Let the sugar cook until it begins to turn amber colored.

In the meantime, combine the black garlic milk with the heavy cream in a saucepan and set it over medium-low heat. Heat it until the liquid is warm to the touch.

When the sugar is a deep amber color, remove the pot from the heat and add the warm milk mixture in a slow, steady stream, whisking constantly. This is when the mixture can bubble up, so be careful. When the milk mixture is incorporated, put the pot back over medium-low heat. Whisk in the powdered milk, xanthan gum, and salt.

In a bowl, lightly beat the eggs. Temper them by whisking in a spoonful of the hot milk mixture. Add the eggs to the pot and whisk to blend. Turn the heat to low and slowly bring the mixture up to 173°F, stirring the bottom of the pot often with a rubber spatula. Remove the pot from the heat and let cool slightly. Transfer the mixture to a container and refrigerate until it's chilled all the way through, at least a couple of hours.

Strain the mixture through a fine-mesh sieve and taste it. Adjust as needed; you might need more maple syrup or a squeeze of lemon juice. Don't be afraid to over-season—food loses a little flavor when it's served very cold or very hot. Pour the mixture into an ice cream maker and follow the instructions on the machine.

* Xanthan gum is a natural sugar that's used as a thickener or a stabilizer. Here, it makes a gelato with a nice, creamy texture and strong, clean flavor. You can find xanthan gum in the baking section of some supermarkets and online.

lemon zest granita

This, of course, is perfectly great all on its own. But as part of the parsley cake dessert, it contributes a very nice citrusy contrast to all the caramel and ginger.

In a small saucepan, heat the water, sugar, and a pinch of salt over medium-low heat until the sugar is dissolved. Let it cool. Put the lemon zest in a loaf pan. Strain the lemon juice through a fine-mesh strainer into the loaf pan and add the sugar water; stir briefly to combine. Put the loaf pan in the freezer.

Over the course of 2½ to 3 hours, stir the mixture with a whisk every 30 to 45 minutes. As it begins to go from slushy to icy, use a fork to stir and scrape it. When the mixture is about the texture of a snow cone, the granita is done. It will keep, covered, in the freezer for a week.

**MAKES 480 GRAMS
(ABOUT 2 CUPS)**

120 grams (½ cup) water

70 grams (generous ⅓ cup) sugar

Kosher salt

Grated zest of 2 lemons

225 grams (1 cup) freshly squeezed lemon juice (from 5 to 7 lemons)

parsley cake crumble

When the cake is cool, set your oven at the lowest possible setting (if you have a dehydrator, even better—set it to 105°F). Line a sheet pan with parchment paper and spray it with cooking spray. Dry the cake out in the oven for 8 to 10 hours, or in the dehydrator for 12 to 15 hours, until toasted through.

Once they are cool, combine the crumbs with the smashed Rice Krispies, powdered sugar, and salt. Taste and add more sugar or salt as desired. The parsley cake crumbs will keep in an air-tight container in the refrigerator for up to two weeks.

**MAKES 140 GRAMS
(ABOUT 2½ CUPS)**

2 cups crumbled parsley cake (use the edges of the cake first, for 1 cup, then pieces of the cake)

Cooking spray

18 grams (½ cup) Rice Krispies, smashed

45 grams (generous ⅓ cup) powdered sugar

A generous pinch of kosher salt

It's a sign of cynical times that we are often asked if our rooftop garden is a prop. We guess people ask that because, in the years since we built ours, rooftop gardens have become a cool and stylish thing for a restaurant to have. Not at all cynically, we are just as often asked how we manage to grow all the produce for such a busy restaurant. We don't do that. Not even close. At best, 10 percent of what's served at Roberta's is grown here. (The numbers are better at Blanca, next door, because it's a twelve-seat restaurant.) People are surprised and sometimes disappointed by that number. But the reality of urban restaurant gardening is that if the restaurant is successful, and if the garden is a garden, meaning it's vulnerable to pests and weather and every other fact of nature, it's impossible for that garden to supply the quantity, much less the quality and consistency, that a restaurant needs on a daily basis. The cynical guy might then ask, what's the point?

The first and most obvious reason, to us, to grow things is because we cook and serve food and because we have the real estate to do it. Beyond that, the garden is a laboratory for the many insane scientists we have working for us. If we want to harvest red mustard greens when they're tiny and tender, we can do that. If we want to experiment with an herb or an heirloom variety of a vegetable, we can grow it. Recipes and drinks successful and otherwise originate from rogue harvests. If something works, we can grow or order more of it. If it doesn't, we can scrap it. We can change the inventory every year if we want. The garden can be a magical place, where chefs can wander through and ask for things and wishes

can be granted. Except, since it's a garden we're talking about here, when it isn't and they can't. Which is a satisfying exchange to watch.

Another reason for our garden to be is that people love it. Kids in the community visit it to learn about growing vegetables. People love to photograph it. When anyone's traveled from farther away than Manhattan to see us, we know they're going to politely ask if they can sidestep the Garden Closed sign and take a peek at it. And since we expanded the garden into the space next door, covering every viable inch with something living and edible—mountain mint, wild strawberries, Sungold tomatoes, rat's-tail radishes, nasturtiums—people have liked to eat dinner, have parties, get married, and celebrate things in general in there. We think the garden is happier for it.

Some think of Roberta's as the patron saint of rooftop gardening in New York City. We are honored. But we hope the idea of a restaurant having a garden doesn't get romanticized right into fantasyland. We hope it becomes less novel and romantic and more realistic and everyday. We hope it becomes a given that if you have space and you're cooking and serving food, you grow some edible things.

Although we should note: It's not easy. Growing stuff is hard. And because of space and soil and growing conditions and because there aren't volumes written about it like there are with conventional growing, urban gardening is especially hard. We're writing a manual as we go. And we've learned the number one most useful thing you could ever know about growing anything: You have to just plant things and see how they do in the space and the soil that you've got. You can't possibly know what will thrive and what will fail until you do that.

STRAWBERRY SHORTCAKE

angel food, strawberry cream, green granita, tristar strawberry

SERVES 20; ANGEL CAKE
ALONE SERVES 10

Cooking spray or
butter, for greasing
the pan

140 grams (1 cup) all-
purpose flour

70 grams (½ cup plus
2¼ teaspoons)
cornstarch

460 grams (2 cups plus
1 tablespoon) superfine
sugar

8 large egg whites

3.75 grams (1 teaspoon)
cream of tartar

6 grams (2 teaspoons)
kosher salt

5 grams (generous
1 teaspoon) vanilla
extract

Strawberry cream
(recipe follows)

Green granita (recipe
follows)

Fresh strawberries,
preferably Tristars,
washed and stemmed

Despite what the recipes in this chapter might lead you to believe, our original pastry chef Katy Peetz is not a huge fan of cake. She *is* a huge fan of angel food cake. Her version is moister and chewier—in a good way—than the supermarket versions you might have had. It makes a soft, not-too-sweet bed for the best strawberries summertime has to offer. And before you turn the whole thing into the edible version of a tumble in a strawberry patch, she recommends eating the crispy edges of the cake the second it comes out of the oven. They're not the same once they've cooled.

Preheat the oven to 350°F. Spray the bottom only of a 9- x 13-inch baking pan that's at least 1½ inches deep with cooking spray or grease it with butter, and lay parchment paper over that. Spray or lightly butter the parchment. Do not spray or butter the sides of the pan. Set two loaf pans upside down a few inches apart from each other on your counter. (You'll put the cake upside down in its pan on top of these when it comes out of the oven. It will keep its volume while it cools, instead of deflating. If you don't do this, or if you do and it falls anyway, that's okay; the cake will taste the same.)

Sift the flour and cornstarch into a medium bowl and add 310 grams (1⅓ cups) of the superfine sugar; stir to combine.

In a stand mixer fitted with the whisk attachment, start beating the egg whites on low speed. Add the cream of tartar and salt, and continue beating until the mixture looks foamy, with very tiny bubbles. Add the vanilla and increase the mixer speed to medium. Gradually add the remaining 150 grams (⅔ cup plus 1 tablespoon) superfine sugar. After about 2 minutes, when the mixture has doubled in size, gradually add

the flour mixture. Just before the flour is completely incorporated, stop the mixer and remove the bowl. Using a rubber spatula, give the mixture a few good circular stirs, making sure to scoop the batter at the bottom of the bowl up to the top. This is an airy cake and you want to keep it that way; don't stir any more than a few times. Pour the batter immediately into the lined sheet pan and put it in the oven.

Check the cake after 40 minutes. It should be golden brown and the sides should be beginning to pull away from the pan. Insert a cake tester; it should come out clean. If it doesn't, bake it for 5 more minutes. Pull the pan from the oven and turn it over onto your loaf pan "pillars." Let it cool. Wrapped in plastic, the cake will keep for two to three days. If your kitchen is warm, keep it in the refrigerator. The cake will sink a little, but it will still taste good.

To serve, tear the inside of the angel food cake—not the corners— into square-ish pieces; you'll use 2 to 3 small pieces per serving. Put 2 spoonfuls of strawberry cream on each plate and follow it with the cake. Scatter a spoonful of green granita over the cake, and garnish each plate with a small handful of strawberries.

strawberry cream

Strawberry cream is just strawberry puree with whipped cream folded into it. This recipe makes more than you need. It's a precious condiment. Use it on ice cream, yogurt, oatmeal, or just eat it with a spoon straight out of the container.

300 grams (1 pint) strawberries, preferably small, juicy ones like Tristars

80 grams (6½ tablespoons) sugar

Juice of ½ lemon

115 grams (½ cup) heavy cream

2 grams (¼ teaspoon) kosher salt

28 grams (2 tablespoons) crème fraîche (page 109) or sour cream

Wash, stem, and halve the strawberries. In a bowl, toss them with the sugar and lemon juice. Cover the bowl and let it sit in the refrigerator overnight or for up to two days.

When you're ready to make the puree, strain the liquid from the strawberries and put it in a saucepan over medium-low heat. Bring the liquid to a simmer and let it reduce to a syrup, 8 to 10 minutes. Add the strawberries to the syrup and give it a good stir. Cook the mixture at a simmer for another 5 to 10 minutes, stirring and scraping the bottom of the saucepan with a rubber spatula. You want the mixture to have a thick but just short of jammy consistency.

Remove the saucepan from the heat and add a pinch of salt. Let the mixture cool, and then transfer it to a blender. Puree on high speed for 1 to 2 minutes. Transfer it to the refrigerator until well chilled. The puree will keep in the refrigerator for up to a week; you can also freeze it for up to three months.

To make the whipped cream, using a hand mixer, whip the heavy cream on low speed, gradually increasing it to high, until very soft peaks begin to form. Add the salt and crème fraîche or sour cream, and mix on high speed for 30 more seconds.

To make the strawberry cream, put the strawberry puree in a bowl and fold the whipped cream into it, using a rubber spatula.

green granita

Use whatever greens you like for this—Katy throws in whatever's growing in the garden that's not pretty enough to be served on a plate. Just make sure it's not too sweet—it's meant to be a bright, slightly bitter counterpoint to all the sweetness of the strawberry shortcake.

Make sure all your ingredients are cold, except for the sweetened condensed milk, which should be at room temperature. If the greens and celery aren't cold, chill them in the refrigerator for an hour before using. (If the juice for the granita gets warm, it will begin to turn brown.)

Put a few small ice cubes into a loaf pan. In a juicer, juice the watercress, parsley, celery, and apple. Strain the liquid through a fine-mesh sieve into the loaf pan, along with the juice of half a lemon. Immediately whisk in the sweetened condensed milk. Add a pinch of salt. Taste, and add more salt or lemon juice if needed. Transfer the pan to the freezer. Over the course of 2½ to 3 hours, stir the mixture with a whisk every 30 to 45 minutes. As it begins to go from slushy to icy, use a fork to stir and scrape it. When the mixture is about the texture of a snow cone, the granita is done. It will keep, covered, in the freezer for a week.

**MAKES 480 GRAMS
(2 CUPS)**

150 grams (4 tightly packed cups) mix of watercress (ends trimmed) and parsley (leaves only)

3 celery ribs, plus a small handful celery leaves

1 Granny Smith apple, cored, diced, and tossed in the juice of half a lemon and chilled in the refrigerator

1 lemon

20 grams (1½ tablespoons) sweetened condensed milk

Kosher salt

GELATO COOKIES

MAKES ABOUT 4 CUPS
COOKIES

These cookies were engineered to taste like bits of sugar cone. They are addictive with or without gelato.

4 large egg whites, at room temperature

1.5 grams (½ teaspoon) kosher salt

85 grams (¾ cup) powdered sugar

85 grams (½ cup minus 1 heaping tablespoon) sugar

60 grams (4¼ table-spoons) unsalted butter, melted

180 grams (1 cup plus 4½ tablespoons) all-purpose flour

Using a stand mixer fitted with the paddle attachment, beat the egg whites, salt, and both of the sugars together on low speed until well combined. Add the melted butter in a slow stream, and increase the speed to medium. Add the flour and mix until there are no lumps, a minute or two. Pour the batter into a small container and let it rest in the refrigerator for up to 1 hour.

Preheat the oven to 325°F. Remove the batter from the fridge. Put 11- x 16-inch silicone baking mats on two sheet pans. Using a small spatula, spread a thin layer of batter onto each mat. The resulting shape doesn't have to be perfect, because you're going to break up the cookies after they're baked, but you want the thickness of the layer to be consistent so it cooks evenly. Bake for 10 to 12 minutes, until the cookies are golden brown. Let cool on the mats until cool enough to handle.

Break the cookies into small to medium pieces, and store them in an airtight container. The cookies will stay crispy for a few days. They also freeze well for up to three months.

SWEET TEA GELATO

At the restaurant, Katy likes to roll this gelato out in early to mid spring. According to her, that's when fresh local produce is still limited but summer is already on everyone's mind. This gelato—made with black tea—offers a taste of it.

MAKES 940 GRAMS
(ABOUT 1 QUART)

700 grams (3 cups) whole milk

Peel from 1 lemon (reserve the lemon)

62 grams (generous ¼ cup) loose black tea, preferably White Heron

565 grams (2½ cups) heavy cream

187 grams (¾ cup plus 2 teaspoons) sugar

37 grams (2½ table-spoons) honey

50 grams (⅓ cup plus 1 tablespoon) powdered milk

3 grams (generous ½ teaspoon) xanthan gum (see note, page 256)

3 grams (scant ¾ teaspoon) kosher salt

1 large egg

1 egg yolk

In a medium saucepan, combine the milk, lemon peel, and black tea leaves. Place the saucepan over medium-low heat, cover it, and bring the liquid to a simmer. When the liquid begins to bubble, turn off the heat and let it sit for 20 minutes. Strain the milk mixture through a fine-mesh sieve set over a bowl, and discard the tea leaves and lemon peel.

In a saucepan, combine the tea-infused milk with the cream and bring the liquid to a simmer over medium heat. Turn heat to low and add the sugar, honey, powdered milk, xanthan gum, and salt, whisking gently to combine. Turn off the heat.

In a large bowl, lightly beat the egg and yolk. Temper them by whisking in a spoonful of the hot cream mixture. Add the eggs to the saucepan and whisk to blend. Set the pan over low heat and slowly bring the mixture up to 173°F, stirring the bottom of the pan often with a rubber spatula. Remove the pan from the heat.

Using an immersion blender, preferably, or a hand mixer, blend the mixture for 1 minute. Then transfer it to a container and refrigerate until it's chilled all the way through, at least a couple of hours.

Remove the chilled mixture from the refrigerator and whisk in the juice of half the reserved lemon. Strain it through a fine-mesh sieve, pour it into an ice cream maker, and follow the instructions on the machine.

WATERCRESS GELATO

MAKES 1.15 KILOGRAMS
(1½ QUARTS)

940 grams (1 quart) whole milk

400 grams (14 ounces) trimmed watercress, washed

332 grams (scant 1½ cups) heavy cream

200 grams (1 cup) sugar

75 grams (3½ table-spoons) honey

100 grams (¾ cup) powdered milk

3 grams (generous ½ teaspoon) xanthan gum (see note, page 256)

4 grams (½ teaspoon) kosher salt

2 large eggs, at room temperature

Juice of half a lemon

When there's an abundance of green things at the farmers' markets and in our garden, green inevitably spills over into our desserts. This gelato is clean tasting, bright, and a little peppery—it's our favorite. But besides watercress, we've also used chamomile, lemon verbena, basil, and mint. The only rules of thumb here are: (1) Use really fresh herbs, (2) don't overcook them, and (3) figure on 400 to 500 grams of herbs per 1 batch of gelato base. Have fun.

Combine the milk with 200 grams of the watercress in a pot and place it over medium-low heat. Bring it to a simmer, cover, and let barely simmer—there should be no bubbling—for 40 minutes. Remove the pot from the heat and let the milk cool. Strain the milk through a fine-mesh sieve and discard the watercress.

In a saucepan, combine 150 grams (⅔ cup) of the watercress milk with the cream and bring the liquid to a simmer over medium heat. Turn the heat to low and add the sugar, honey, powdered milk, xanthan gum, and salt, whisking gently to combine. Turn off the heat.

Prepare an ice bath in a big container, such as a deep rectangular Tupperware. In a bowl, lightly beat the eggs. Temper them by whisking in a spoonful of the hot cream mixture. Add the eggs to the saucepan and whisk to blend. Set the pan over low heat and slowly bring the mixture up to 173°F, stirring the bottom of the pan often with a rubber spatula. Remove from the heat and transfer to a bowl. Put the remaining 200 grams of watercress in the bowl with the base. Set the bowl over the ice bath.

Using an immersion blender, preferably, or a hand mixer, blend the mixture for 1 minute. Then transfer it to a container and refrigerate until it's chilled all the way through, at least a couple of hours.

Remove the chilled mixture from the refrigerator and whisk in the
lemon juice. Strain it through a fine-mesh sieve, pour it into an ice
cream maker, and follow the instructions on the machine.

DRINKS

The history of drink-making at Roberta's is long and populous. If there's such a thing as too many cooks in the kitchen—and there is—we've yet to see it hold true for bartenders. Most of these cocktails are the result of a collaborative effort, as are the descriptions and "Recommend If You Like" notes—RIYL—that accompany them. Rather than mess with those, we've left them as is—just as you'd find them if you were working behind the bar at Roberta's.

From left to right: Cannery Row, La Bardot, Dean's Dream, American Nightmare, and Boston Pea Party

american nightmare SERVES 1

2 whole cloves

2 lemon quarters

2 ounces Booker's bourbon

1 ounce Vergano Americano*

½ ounce Grand Marnier

Orange bitters

Big ice cubes

This drink is a classic from the earliest days of Roberta's. It was designed to showcase the alcoholic intensity (128 proof) of Booker's bourbon, not to cover it up. RIYL: Old-fashioneds, one-night stands, hangovers.

In a cocktail shaker, muddle the cloves and lemon quarters. Add the bourbon, Vergano Americano, Grand Marnier, a dash of orange bitters, and 4 big ice cubes. Close the shaker and give it a vigorous eight-count shake.

Rinse a rocks glass with orange bitters and fill it with 3 big ice cubes.

Strain the drink into the glass and serve.

* This is a fortified wine from northern Italy that's worth seeking out. It's like a spicy, bittersweet sweet vermouth.

boston pea party SERVES 1

3 or 4 fresh snap peas

2 ounces Plymouth gin

½ ounce fresh lemon juice

½ ounce simple syrup (recipe follows)

Big ice cubes

Freshly ground black pepper

This is, of course, a seasonal cocktail. We don't do a lot of overtly seasonal cocktails because being all overt about seasonality isn't really our style. But this drink reappears on the menu every summer—with snap peas either from our garden or from Satur Farms on Long Island. RIYL: Mojitos, Caipirinhas, Wiffle ball in the park.

In a cocktail shaker, combine the snap peas, gin, lemon juice, and simple syrup. Add 4 big ice cubes to the shaker and close it.

Fill a rocks glass with 3 big ice cubes. Give the shaker a vigorous eight-count shake. Pour (do not strain) the drink into the glass. Give the drink a grind of black pepper and serve.

simple syrup MAKES 340 GRAMS (1½ CUPS)

225 grams (1 cup) water

200 grams (1 cup) sugar

Combine the water and sugar in a small saucepan and set it over high heat. Bring to a boil and let simmer for 3 minutes, until the sugar is dissolved. Remove from the heat and let cool. The simple syrup will keep in a glass container in the refrigerator for up to a month.

dean's dream SERVES 1

1½ ounces Milagro tequila

1 ounce white vermouth

½ ounce mescal

1 ounce fresh lime juice

½ ounce honey simple syrup (recipe follows)

Big ice cubes

Pernod

Freshly ground black pepper

So, inevitably, this is a cocktail whose name has no real meaning. One of our bartenders just really liked the name of a Dead Milkmen song, and rightly thought it had a nice ring to it. RIYL: Margaritas, Mescal Gimlets, the Cheesus Christ.

In a cocktail shaker, combine the tequila, vermouth, mescal, lime juice, and honey simple syrup with 4 big ice cubes.

Rinse a rocks glass with Pernod and fill it with 3 big ice cubes. Give the shaker a vigorous eight-count shake and strain the drink into the rocks glass.

Garnish with a grind of black pepper and serve.

honey simple syrup MAKES 540 GRAMS (ABOUT 2 CUPS)

320 grams (1 cup) honey

225 grams (1 cup) water

Put the honey in a small saucepan and set it over medium heat. When the honey is warm, add the water and stir until well combined. Remove from the heat and let cool. The honey simple syrup will keep in a glass container in the refrigerator for up to a month.

la bardot SERVES 1

This is a drink with curves—soft, citrusy Lillet, smooth gin, and a little bit of a bite. The name just fit. RIYL: Gin and Tonics, Gin 'n' Juice, girls.

In a cocktail shaker, gently muddle 2 of the shiso leaves with 3 dashes of sriracha bitters. Add the gin, Lillet, and citrus juice along with 4 big ice cubes.

Fill a rocks glass with 3 big ice cubes. Give the shaker a vigorous eight-count shake and strain the drink into the glass. Top with a splash of tonic, garnish with a shiso leaf, and serve.

3 shiso leaves

Sriracha bitters*

1 ounce Beefeater gin

1 ounce Lillet Blanc**

1 ounce fresh Cara Cara orange juice or tangerine juice

Big ice cubes

Tonic

* A company called Brooklyn Hemispherical Bitters makes these bitters, which are, of course, spicy. You can get them at some gourmet food shops on the East and West Coasts, and online.

** Lillet Blanc is a French aperitif made from a blend of wine and citrus liqueurs. On its own, well-chilled or on the rocks, it makes for light, easy drinking.

cannery row SERVES 1

2 ounces Old Overholt rye

1 ounce Cynar*

½ ounce fresh lemon juice

A splash of simple syrup (page 274)

Big ice cubes

Ginger beer

Orange bitters

1 orange

A sprig of rosemary

* Cynar is a bitter Italian liqueur with potent herbaceous flavor. It makes a killer digestif served with a splash of soda and a twist of lemon or just solo, on the rocks.

This cocktail is a refined version of one of our longtime bartenders' personal go-to drinks. It's dark, spicy, and a little bitter. RIYL: Dark 'n' Stormies, Whiskey Sours, bartenders from Maine.

In a cocktail shaker, combine the rye, Cynar, lemon juice, and simple syrup, and add 4 big ice cubes.

Fill a rocks glass with 3 big ice cubes. Stir the mixture in the shaker vigorously and strain into the glass. Top with a splash of ginger beer.

Add a dash of orange bitters, garnish with a twist of orange and the rosemary, and serve.

One way to survive being indoctrinated into the New York City restaurant scene with your sanity and your integrity reasonably intact is to keep changing. We may have had to come on the grid and to conform to some conventions. We may have had to polish the experience of eating at the restaurant so that it wasn't a total shock to the average system. We are glad for that. We weren't trying to piss anyone off—least of all the people who traveled a long way to eat at our restaurant. But as we went about smoothing rough edges and building an infrastructure and all that increasingly necessary work, we were simultaneously finding other outlets for freedom and anarchy. We minded the shop and we expanded our borders across the backyard and into other parts of the city and other parts of the country. We found new places to throw parties and new rooftops to build on and we took our show on the road.

Eventually we took over the next-door space and built a restaurant that almost no one could have ever imagined us building. So we may have fallen in line (everything is relative) but we aren't going to stop growing. We are going to remain the kind of place where you might have been once, but you have absolutely no idea what is going to be happening there the next time you come back.

SOURCES

00 flour, 'nduja, bottarga (we use bottarga di muggine, or mullet; not tonno, tuna), **Pecorino Fiore Sardo, Taleggio, burrata, straciatella, cured meat,** and all kinds of other Italian ingredients can be found at Buon Italia, www.buonitalia.com. Two exceptions are **vin cotto,** which is available from a few online sources, and **gran blu di bufala,** which you can find at Murray's Cheese, www.murrayscheese.com. **Fresh black truffle** can be ordered from almagourmet.com and other online purveyors.

Caputo Brothers mozzarella curd is sold at Saxelby Cheese, saxelbycheese.com. **Prairie Breeze Cheddar, roomano pradera,** and other excellent cheeses can be found at Murray's Cheese, www.murrayscheese.com. **Salvatore Bklyn smoked ricotta** (www.salvatorebklyn .com) is sold at Whole Foods markets in New York City, and is otherwise available from Saxelby Cheese.

You can get **shichimi togarashi, fennel pollen,** and other harder-to-find spices from kalustyans.com.

Kombu and **bonito flakes** are easily found at Asian markets, some bigger supermarkets, and online. **Ayu fish sauce** is harder to find. Some intrepid Internet searching will turn it up, but you may have to contact a specialty retailer like True World Foods to inquire about purchasing. A good substitute for it, Red Boat Fish Sauce, is available at Asian markets and online. **Black garlic** can be found at blackgarlic.com.

American caviar and **trout roe** are available from Caviar Russe, caviarrusse.com. The best way to get **sea urchin** is to ask for it at the best fish market you can find. **Maine shrimp,** when in season, can be ordered from Harbor Fish Market, harborfish.com.

D'Artagnan, dartagnan.com, is a reliable source for **squab, guinea hen, duck fat, venison,** and other hard-to-find-at-the-supermarket animal products. River & Glen, riverandglen.com, is another good source for squab. The **wild rice** we serve with the guinea hen is from Bineshii, bineshiiwildrice.com. You can get **Poulet Rouge** from Joyce Farms, joycefoods.com.

Benton's bacon can be found at www.bentons countryhams2.com. Accept no substitutes.

Heritage Foods, heritagefoodsusa.com, has **double-cut pork chops, ground pork,** and other quality meat from heritage breeds. You can get **Mangalitsa pork collar** from Mosefund Farm, mosefundfarm.com. **Foie gras** can be ordered from Hudson Valley Foie Gras, hudsonvalleyfoiegras.com.

ACKNOWLEDGMENTS

CARLO MIRARCHI: I'd like to thank my mother, father, and brother. For everything. BRANDON HOY: To my beautiful, loving family and my halfway decent friends. CHRIS PARACHINI: Mom for bringing me in, Dad for showing me the ropes, Georgia for catching a fire. KATHERINE WHEELOCK: Thank you, Jim and Luke, for being beyond. And the Wheelock, MacLachlan, Scordamaglia, and Veitch families for endless help and support. Thank you, Kim and Allison. Thanks to Rica and Marysarah and the Clarkson Potter team. To Kenji. To Ryan Rice. To recipe testers Jill Santopietro, Amy Vogler, and Stacy Adimando for incredible patience and meticulousness. To everyone at Roberta's but especially Tom, Vanessa, Kip, and Cherie for being so awesome. And Meg and David for all their help. And Katy. And Lauren. And Anthony. And Gabe. And thank you, Carlo and Chris and Brandon, for everything.

INDEX

BREAD